S C000192722 ıl:
ıe

copyright

Sounds of the Soul: Adventures in Time, Andrea Waddell
Published by Scribbulations LLC
www.scribbulations.com
ISBN 978-1-935751-00-7

Front cover photo by Ben Hawley. Back cover photo by Lee Towsey.

suggestion

If after reading Andrea's poems you would consider making a donation in her name to a cause which was very close to her heart, may we suggest The Lord Dowding Fund for Humane Research, which awards grants for medical and scientific research without the use of animals.

The Lord Dowding Fund for Humane Research
Millbank Tower,
Millbank,
London SW1P 4QP
(Tel: 020 7630 3340)
www.ldf.org.uk

vocabulary

Andrea had a rich and varied vocabulary, and so you will find at the back a glossary of some of the more unusual words she has used.

contents

foreword

Andrea died tragically at the age of 29, but those short years were crammed full of diverse experiences, all of which are hinted at in her poetry.

She studied Philosophy at the University of Durham, and later completed an MA in Social and Political Thought at the University of Sussex, all the while suffering severely from fibromyalgia (which is a syndrome of problems including painful muscles, abdominal problems, sleeplessness and depression). The constant pain often meant that it was impossible for her to carry shopping or textbooks, to stay for long in any one position, or even brush her hair or hold a telephone to her ear. (She always found ways round these problems: for instance, she would visit a local hairdresser each day, and for 50p they would brush her hair for her!)

After achieving her degrees, Andrea decided to study massage and aromatherapy and, in spite of her painful muscles, she was able to give massages which the recipients always found amazingly beneficial. Later on she went out to Thailand on two separate occasions, for several weeks at a time, to study for diplomas in all the various Thai massage techniques.

Her life reads like a catalogue of challenges and difficulties. She was anorexic in childhood, then diagnosed with scoliosis, later developing the fibromyalgia mentioned above. She was bullied at school, knocked down by a car in Battersea, mugged in Prague (where she was teaching English in her gap year), and once was attacked by a gang of young thugs in Reading. While completing her second degree she developed acute ulcerative colitis which was nearly fatal, but she underwent a successful operation resulting in an ileostomy, which was later reversed. It was also at this time that her lifelong gender dysphoria was resolved surgically. In spite of all these vicissitudes Andrea never lost her zest for life and her sense of humour, and indeed she seemed to become stronger and more concerned for others as a result of every situation in which she found herself.

Andrea loved music (classical was her especial joy) and going to concerts; and she enjoyed visiting art galleries. She read voraciously (she was still working her way through the final volumes of Proust!); and she practised yoga and worked-out at the gym to keep her painful muscles under some sort of control. She was also studying Spanish; and she refused to own a television!

She was hailed on one internet site after her death as a 'vegan animal activist', and she did indeed work tirelessly for animals. However, she was also vitally interested in people, and always wanted to help anyone who was disadvantaged in life.

We knew Andrea wrote poetry, but it was not until after her death that her brother found the complete opus of poems on her laptop, composed between 2003 and 2009 and already arranged into groups (the headings are all Andrea's), and with her Preamble already written, in typical Andrea style! We, her family, are very happy to now complete Andrea's task and finally to publish her poems. We are very grateful to those special friends and members of Andrea's family who have each contributed comments on some of the poems.

Andrea was beautiful and brave, witty and clever, funny and (definitely) scatty. She was a private person, trying to be independent in spite of all her problems, and never complaining about the hand which Life had dealt her. We think that everyone she came into contact with, in whatever walk of life, went away feeling better, inspired, touched by her light. We are so proud of her.

Andrea's family.

preamble

Philosophy is finished. The futility of seeking to assume the mantle of a wholly universalised, impersonalised voice, (that construction designated by the darling 'reason' of philosophers, with which we might rather say that, in their conceit, they *presume* to speak) has been rudely exposed in the history of its making and its demise (though the failure of a grand dream does not prohibit living on in denial, which is of course all-too-typical of dreaming). Despite its natural nobility, in seeing itself exempt from the ordinary obligation to appeal to people's sensibilities, philosophy killed their desire to believe in its own pronouncements, to inhabit their visceral essence and so feel swept along by their vital power. In consequence, the *l'enfant terrible* within people's souls never tired of seeking out the hidden paradox, through its self-appointed role as a devil's advocate, an activity which has always had all the stature of a parlour game.

Well, just as the practice of poetry pre-dated the birth of philosophy, let us all become poets once again! The spirit of philosophy will always burn in the living soul. Poetry, then, is the vehicle for the continuation of philosophy by other means. The secret ingredient of my collection has been a radically subjective viewpoint. I do not believe in the possibility of expounding totally impersonal and objective universal truths. I grapple with ultimate concerns and I treat this grappling as a form of art in itself. I appeal to the authority of my own subjective avowals as the only veridical security I should ever need.

My methodological dictum has been to avoid any reference to the 'real world' as commonly understood. In some of my pieces I actually seek to problematise the very notion of a 'real world' or 'external reality'. It is my belief that poetry must strive to capture that primordial sense of unitary experience – something of which we are all dimly aware yet all too often feel ourselves forced to disregard.
I wanted to prove the very possibility of such a project, bound by such

a stricture. Yet where it may be said that I have deviated from this stricture, I intend that the particular worldly artefacts alluded to must be seen as naked, devoid of context, and absurd, rather in the manner of Marcel Duchamp's "readymades" (the classic example of which being the ordinary urinal put on a pedestal and summarily declared as art).

Obversely, each concept I invoke might be interpreted as deriving from that aforementioned "real world", yet I want to display it naked, divorced from the myriad contexts which sully it every time, always waylaying our attention and skewing it towards that "real world". I, on the contrary, want to showcase the possibility of beholding real meaning. A word is the ultimate conceptual minimalism. I want each word to do the maximum work made possible by its pure form, so as to yield its maximal cognitive distillate. For a word in nudeness can evoke more than the greatest of poets is able to, in seeking to string a collection of them together. I like to lean on the barest of metres, often incorporating just a two-stress pattern, which allows maximum stress to be placed on the individual words.

My words and metaphors thus become larger-than-life; my poems are surreal. This is not supposed to be a slur on their truthfulness. Their surrealism is the tool with which I seek to achieve this goal and draw the purest of pictures before the mind's eyes. They are literally "not of this world". But suffice to say I had no intention of writing "science-fiction". Yet the pedant who insists on picking apart my poems with his analytical scalpel will no doubt delight in proving their lack of everyday meaning.

The possibility of meaning likewise becomes an urgent problematic in light of my rejection of the possibility of universal truths. We have a whole battery of cognitive protocols which allow us to put to trial any assertion which presumes to claim special significance for itself and spurns our usual everyday hermeneutic contexts.

A poem, then, is something whose beauty of form alone allows it to say the unsayable. We freely circumvent our normal protocols of cognitive validity when in the presence of beauty of form. It is obviously churlish to put beauty under the knife. Yet we also positively demand the beautiful to be meaningful, in contradistinction to the pronouncements of philosophy which we commonly delight in subverting. (And if it happens that we don't find that beauty, there is clearly nothing to be gained from dissection).

This, then, has been, my ultimate, but humble, criterion for my poetic creations: that yielded by the desire to create something beautiful. At the same time, creation must be tempered by destruction. I have pruned each poem to its bare foundations, so that it might function quite apart from any secret intentions with which I might have overlaid it in my mind. I want each poem to be about the words themselves, and not at all about the artist, so that each word might set specific mental cogs moving for the reader. We can marvel at their play. Each poem is a little machine. Perhaps the only meaning to be found in them at all lies in their aesthetic form, if by meaning is demanded something potentially other than the words used (until we branch off in our own particular reverie). I don't pretend to any kind of intellectual rigour which would stand sceptical scrutiny outside the magic circle of my own poetic reveries.

I spurn empirical and narrative poetry, or rather: I re-forge it according to my methodological requirements. In the main, though, it seems to me that the poetic pre-occupation with the doings of other people and with the material realm betrays a fear of revealing our own soul and confronting our own demons. Similarly, narrative literature so easily misses the critical dynamics governing the heart of the life-process. For the thinner we spread ourselves in narrating events, the blinder we will be to disclosing the ultimate dynamic of 'real experience'.

Yet just as in the 'deep empiricism' of an introspective, subjective standpoint which allows me to find a voice where the pedantry of analytical philosophy struggles to speak at all (though it lives in denial) - time, nonetheless, manifests itself as my ultimate and insurmountable adversary. Because I can only recount my critical impressions through time, they will always be temporally indexed. While I can claim a certain 'sincerity in the moment', here lies the root of my ultimate doubts regarding my poetic veracity.

With a simple crank of time's screw, our deepest convictions can evaporate or be up-ended. This uncertainty goes to the heart of the poetic form as I understand it. Each of my poems may be thought to involve a dialectical movement. This may be a critical dynamic between fulfilment and despair, or more fundamentally: between grasping at a nugget of truth and watching it seep away; between upholding the very possibility of meaning and yielding to the infinite and eternal void.

Yet the very concrete form is then disingenuous. For a poem has a beginning, a middle, and an end. Yet time may not be so easily divided. Thus in insinuating the form of a conclusion, by one lookout I may have inadvertently turned truth on its head, for the flow of time is seamless and inexorable. It is futile to seek to determine in good faith where a poem should begin, and where it should end, or, *pari passu*, to seek to adjudicate between the causes of optimism and pessimism.

Andrea Waddell

May 2007

psychology

an epic of sorts

behind the
simple-minded
peace and quiet
of the same-old psychic sound
of here and now

lies a parallel spiritual realm
untold till now but most profound
(but behold)
this bloody internecine drama
is ready to come flooding
hither into the otherwise vacant mind
with its apocalyptic flicker

this dead-weight of guilt -
a penance each moment bestowed
from not excelling in effort -
is sinking my ship;
of course, it's all in my mind -
unveridical apparitions -
yet how I fidget
as I listen
to the dripping of time

(follow on: This Human Zoo / Other Souls)

Andrea Waddell

ars vivendi

when I'm feeling macho
my conscience resolves
to labour life into shape
with the sweat of my brow
and the thwacks of a hammer

whilst I bash this way and that
in the hephaestian fire
and I make bold to apply the lash
to the sasquatch of life,
in blood-thirsty *aleithia,*
by my imagined god-anointed right,
I descry phantasmagoria in liminal vision:
a theophany of life peers down *upon* me
and *mocks* me
from the mists of Olympus

when I submit
to the feminine instinct
I genuflect
before the spinners of fate
who whimsically guide
my roller-coaster ride -
I bow down before infinite power -
now my sole guarantee
is the goodness of me

now if I master
the horse-whispering art,
by a secret reflux motion
life either laps at my feet, very gently
or just respectfully circumvents me

but what if fate takes me
by surprise
with a definitive tsunami?

commentary

This is a great poem. No, I do not mean "great" in the modern throw-away empty meaning for anything that merely exceeds the pass mark of modest expectations, but monumentally great—like a standing stone in literature. It is no poetic lollypop, but stern stuff. It requires work on the reader's part to decipher and discern the nuances of meaning and classical allusions. But the reward is great—to hear a cri de coeur that cuts to the reader's heart and pours in an iodine tincture of shared pain and hope.

It reminds me of Andrea's physical struggles as she grew up, weight-training and developing physical strength, whilst unknown to us, developing an inner strength born of a titanic struggle within.

A great poem to go back to time and time again—in awe of Andrea's honesty and courage.

Dr Peter Little,
Family friend and godfather to Nick.

chariots of fire

isn't it beguiling
how, whatever the hour
or ones current befuddlement,
life desires printing
with the stamp of existence

even so, must it be said
this incessant coo-cooing is all in my head
for what I fear more
is the sound of the void

in blind emotion
I imbibe truth,
and when I smell
authentic attitude
as a rule I'm
jellified -
it's sexy and it's cool

an attitude bequeaths meaning
by spurring me forward
and marking my path
while surplus detritus
can fall by the verge

its required ocular knowledge
for driving my troika
that all's paradisiacal
upon the horizon

when I'm caught off my mettle
my attitude-carrying steed
feels like a fraudulent cripple,
no more than a
confidence trickster -
now reality imprints me
with its whistling enigma

missive

here's my missive
to all infinite space
notwithstanding
any passing members
(and all conscious embers)
of the human race

my soul abides in a humble bubble
- though it boasts
simplicity of taste
notwithstanding
it's warm and snug
and fit for any king

it's fitted up
with darkened glass
- whilst I gaze out
all passers-by
just hearken past

the stream of house-keeping
demanded by diurnal living
and dealing with the environs of rubble
tolls unceasing trouble
and psychic strife
- this soul can count herself
full-time housewife and mother

my mind steals peeks at

the great blue yonder
idly guessing at
its secrets
and wonders
- it's the jilted life of reason

all the while my bubble drifts
through time and circumstance
my myopic, homely soul
confounds the new with happenstance -
quite oblivious to "Iraq"

commentary

We all have a bit of the spirit of Andrea within us. It is that nagging little voice that wants us to escape from our conventional life and become free.

I was privileged to see the metamorphosis of Alex into the beautiful butterfly that became Andrea. I had no idea she wrote poetry, but in a way I am not surprised.

I wish I could use words as she did.

Steve Allen,
Consultant in Pain Management, Reading and Oxford Hospitals.

bungie in the jungle

trudging deeper and deeper
through this jungle undergrowth
sunlight evades me
while this crepuscule drags asunder
soul with body

I'm like a botanist transfixed
by the plethora of sensory specimens admixed;
scents tease my head,
and magnetise my mind,
like an animal bewitched -
and thinking flits like fireflies' tricks -
while the enswirling river of Lethe
purges thought of my brief,
thus expunging all remembrance
of my mental direction

yet in the midst of this dream
thought switches on and off like a beam -
my secret bungee cord extracts me
and yanks me sky-high –
then I espy the whole of my life,
then may I recollect
I am living my life
and should proceed with swiftness forthwith.
I perceive too the delicate stream
where unerringly
reality meets dreams

philosophy of the forenoon

when I wake from mental slumbers
and the vernal tips of spring rear their heads above the barren
clod
I feel the breath of primal gods;
falls athwart the undergrowth their looming shadow.

I sense the tickle of gossamer threads
quite blind to the whereabouts of the spider's den;
I feel the call of primal lust
but my vision's still clogged from the sandman's dust

to be sure, the great mass of humanity slumbers and sleepwalks
through the seas of reality,
while the noble arrow of time just flutters away to some faraway
secret land,
and the great frozen structures of past present and future
melt away into one puddle,
leaving only the gnashing of clocks

from the standpoint of living I
cast my eyes back on my slumbers as ever so queer,
incredulous they starred me,
and just puzzled at the holes in my memory
and my biography

beyond mere biological subsistence,
which is a kind of hibernation,
I harbour the unadulterated Will to Live;
though what's really living I've no idea;
but lo, did I catch a glimpse in my rear-view mirror?
for I'm really quite bowled over

by the spectacle of life's busy little bees
and stirred by their saccharine
aroma

though I'm still none the wiser
as to the most fitting direction for life, I foresee that
with an effusion of energy will life unfold in its own sweet style;
if I act as inspiration strikes me
I can follow its tributaries
forever buoyed up by trust in the divine,
rather than always wallowing
in the hypothetical life

---

commentary

Life is initially likened to a single day, the forenoon being young adulthood, awakening from the early preoccupations of childhood, and then cleverly switching to the seasonal cycle of a year. The springtime awakening from hibernation matches the emergence of humanity from the fog of pre-existence, or even pre-incarnation, with unfocussed promptings and yearnings, which are all too often stifled by the mind-blocks of adult life. The vector of life is thwarted and time itself is dissipated – I love the gnashing of the clocks! But, Andrea asks, where should we aim, how to avoid the seduction of just getting and spending? Maybe, she says, we should simply go with the flow and let the life-force carry us along.

Robin Waddell,
Andrea's father.

reflections on will-power

the human mind is just a muscle
in fact it is no different from any other
yet compared to my hips and my buttocks
it is quite by far the numbest

the human being is a ruefully stubborn creature, it likes routine
yet when I dream, or so it seems, I breeze, I roam
though feet of clay do plant me squarely
inside the margins of my comfort zone

though it soothes from long acquaintance
with age-old woes I do conduct love-hate relations
by and large, it's free from drafts, and well-sequestered -
the only squally blasts from what lies beyond
invariably emanate from the delirious outpourings
of my fevered brain

my comfort zone depicts my world
it's what I know on this here earth
and, what's further,
it adroitly bounds my feel for here and now

at its marge, placards broadcast
the circle of my values
border guards direct me back
to time-worn tracks
thence back to that abode
I've come to call my home

when I mentally go beyond my precious comfort zone
I suffer the pangs of vertigo
would I submit to a freedom unfettered

Andrea Waddell

I envision my tumbling
head over heels and heels over head
in a bottomless pit –
like the fledgling chick baling out of the nest,
would I learn how to flutter
as I drop and I plummet? -

I'd skim o'er the tops
of all human obstacles -
throwing scorn to those demons
so accustomed to ground me
with yon plaintive cry of reality -
with no reason to stop
I'd be carefree as God
and Ascend up to Heaven

it's a sombering thought
when I recover my stomach
that the cornerstone of reality,
in which humanity acts,
is in fact a bedrock of angst

Christopher Robin and Pooh

bump bump bump
like a sack of spuds -
she jolts and thuds -
she cannot bolt, or flee
all the while she resides
courtesy of the divine majesty
under lock and key.
My physical body
cleaves a path straight and true
through the air
just like Christopher Robin pulling Pooh
down the stairs

how my heart bleeds
as it yields
to the sensory drip-feed
of raw and unrefined
unremitting reality -
I'm like the princess with the pea

my soul blanches
when she espies the horizon;
freezes
when she thinks of infinity

I sing her a lullaby -
now she gently rolls
on the open road -
now we're plodding along
taking life one step at a time

dare I mention
in whispers
my twisted wish
to abort her -
then I'd be hardened and blunt
like a mythical adult

dare I mention
lest it made
my beautiful baby
a little big-headed -
her destiny shoulders a quintessential importance
its for her to save me
she's my redemption

---

commentary

I used to call Andrea 'my valiant daughter', as she always showed a brave face to the world and never wanted people to know of the pain and difficulties of her daily life. Reading her poems I begin to understand what lay beneath her brave outer façade, and I catch glimpses of the despair with which she faced a lifetime of pain and physical problems. But she learnt to plod along "one step at a time", accepting that her destiny "shoulders a quintessential importance" for her soul's growth. The poem shows me Andrea facing up to her life with amazing, indomitable courage.

Sonia Waddell,
Andrea's mother.

a tale for two

how she tickles
when I think; I blubber when I blink:
my fantasy friend
feigning forcible fiend

she hides in the hole
where rumination resides,
sensing my story is spun
my façade framed by fate
she changes the channel;
now's an echo in the air

at a twenty to two in a Tuesday's chores
I cried for Queen and Country
and psychic salvation and
capitalisation

Grapple with my Girly Game…
my God.

ode to ice

e'en as we speak
my enfrosted soul
thaws more
in a gold-fish bowl

the icy idea of the ocean
- its ambience
of insentience -
stays cased
in Oblivion

even now does my mind remain
precariously poised
here within
this prescient
unfreedom

even a fish
thinks
of existence;
this bruising epiphany
takes time for adjustance

Wiccan Logic / Wiccan Grace

when at war with the world
I writhe on the floor -
I brace for the diktats of fate -
all the while, the world's secrets hide
firmly furled

I only know
how to blindly survive,
how to kick
in my will
to exist

by secret Wiccan logic
the conflict persists -
all's sleight of hand
and clockwork bureaucracy
in this ethereal land

drifts downwards
with insouciance
a lattice-work
of calmness,
like heavenly
confettied *leaves*

my wearied soul yields
underneath,
while the birds and the bees
rise up resurgent.

commentary

I believe this poem portrays the extreme forces that are put on us in our daily lives and their effect on our inner worlds: Our friends, the world that surrounds us and our daily struggles for survival, the secret logic in contrast with the conflict that still persists with the world today, that is full of unnecessary problems (such as bureaucracy, war, dictatorship). I think Andrea is pointing out the contrast between life and death, and she ends by emphasising how powerful and beautiful life is.

Truly amazing poems.

Zach Ioannou,
Friend of Andrea's.

basic interrogation techniques

when I think
I pose a challenge to the world
in my Guise as Shrink

I throw down the gauntlet
to nature's functioning
and call a halt to its hustle and bustle

after pistol-whipping it, reality,
and holding the gun to its head
I insist that it shan't so much as blink
before it's given me an account of its conduct

I'm strangely distressed
by my failure to unveil
nature's spell

yet despite my submersion
in my mind's world
I can't help observing in the corner of my eye
the graceful flowing-by of time

thus there's an anaesthetic effect upon my brain
from the thrill of practising interrogation
and it dulls my distress with its impotence
and makes the inexorable unfolding of nature
so much easier to stomach

for the ultimate trick in life to get the hang of
is the ability to smooth time's passage

the harpies

as I pick my way over life's skin
and through
its multifarious sinews

I can't help noticing
an uninvited passenger
just like Coleridge's albatross

yet because each journey leg
is always prescribed by necessity
and endowed with reason's stamp
its only proper she should be gagged;

yet she persists in singeing
my mental tendrils
like a very ethereal acid

and to plead 'stress' is now such a cliché;
yet people yomp on unperturbed
without a twist or swerve -
but without collecting evidence from inside their heads
I don't know what they're saying

yet when I take time out
for cud-chewing
my soul's driven to doubting
the wisdom of every footstep;
the stress-harpy
is testing my deepest values

perhaps the above-mentioned devil
can break free into the outer realm
when our mental powers are feeling tired
and there's a tear in the lining

demons lost and found

isn't it funny
how all life's endeavours
seem justified
by a burst of inner quiet?

this stillness
contrasts with
ordinary working conditions

there's a price exacted
for severing the tentacles
of the demons which suffocate my centre;
they must be made to walk the plank;
the soul must thereafter lose all contact,
for that she might move on
they must be starved of oxygen,
and she must suffer
an expurgation
of the experience of pain

now the value of quiet
is wholly lost to the mind
and the soul is suffused
with a discombobulation
and confusion
thus reduced to her senses
she's struck down with a terror

all adrift at sea
sooner or later
she's reacquainted
with her long lost demons

---

commentary

Andrea had an extraordinary ability to give a deeper meaning to an ordinary thought. However, what I remember most vividly about her is that she had already found her own answers to the most important questions. She always had an opinion even when she acknowledged not having one. Her struggle to find stillness in daily life was obvious in *Demons Lost and Found*. However, it is precisely this sense of stillness and inner peace that I remembered the most. Being around Andrea meant that nothing had to be rushed and that there was time to think about important questions and come up with a clever little idea to make sense of it.

Carmen Cacho,
Friend of Andrea's.

the power of rage

when the soul's requirements
are disrespected by life
one's gut instinct
is to wish it out of existence
and replace it
with a sack of potatoes

but when she's had her fill
of humility
and now won't be deceived
by the virtues of meekness
then rage gets a grip

and all the while she's fixated
by the world's failure
rage is unstintingly breathing
fire into her belly
and she feels as if
she can do anything;
it's like a perpetual motion machine

sometimes, though, it backfires
and begins to eat away her insides
or spills over
in a fit of violence

sometimes in a bolt from the blue
the fire goes awol;
and she's left facing up to
the peculiar bruteness
of life's obstacles
in a fit of stupor

commentary

The disconnect between her hopes, her anticipations, and life's response – or lack of it.   Indeed a sack of spuds would be more use than Life. But the mask of anomie soon slips, the frustration builds, anger is rising within, adrenaline is pumping, anything is possible – though this creative rage can also turn inwards, gnawing like a cancer, despair and numbness revisiting. How often in Andrea's life may this cycle have recurred when facing illness and incomprehension – this poignant poem signals that it was all too familiar to her.

Robin Waddell,
Andrea's father.

the emotion tree

when a situation starts to get sticky,
we take a little trip up the lane to the emotion tree
where every apple is succulent and sweet
but also has a label stating which sort it is;
the label actually peels off,
but just one bite offers the prospect
of a one-way trip into the world of the emotion
as marked on the label

it may feel like a once in a lifetime opportunity
as if the whole of life to date has culminated in this emotional
assessment
which, of course, is not very much like a tax assessment;
it's guttural and instinctive,
although we don't doubt for a moment the strength of logic behind
it;
but of course there's a few main brands of emotion (like soft drink)
and I'll stick my neck out and say we've all tasted each one
innumerable times -
god, human beings are boringly predictable

the apple is our passport
to a magical port-hole
very much like the one of lion, the witch and the wardrobe
fame

and very much like in the story of King Midas
once we're living in this secret world
almost everything we finger,
or just so much as brush up against, becomes coloured
by the same variety of paint in question,
and our foreign policy follows Bush's lead
everything is then categorised according to whether or not it's on
our frequency

and if we're in a really bad mood,
then we fancy the idea of an angel flying overhead to sprinkle
angel dust,
but we've already ruled out of court the possibility because we're
in such a bad mood;
even the rabbits and the earth-worms are conspiring against us

but when we're in a nice mood
then we fancy that the sun shines out of our arse
and the world could actually be quite a nice place too,
and we think we sow seeds of eternal joy everywhere we go,
and we'd love recalcitrant sour-pusses, and aggressive lamp-
posts
which might knock into us
just to go and fuck themselves;

and if you fancy telling me I must have a limited vocabulary
I'll have no compunction in slapping you;
this would be wholly out of respect for the Truth,
and by the way just count the number of letters in *recalcitrant*
and *compunction*

the danger of heeding the call of any emotion
and, for an indeterminate period, abandoning the life of reason
we had been secretly cultivating by doing crossword puzzles
is that we might never find our way back to the wardrobe again;
we might have to spend the rest of our life with those particular
glasses on;
or we might be randomly offered a swap for a different pair of
specs
and again and again *ad infinitum* up to death

we might, forsooth, be swanning around somewhere exotic,
because, for instance, we're in love with another member of the
race,
i.e. the species,
but then it all goes pear-shaped
and we'd actually quite fancy being allowed back to boring
normality
but we can't quite let go, because when we've tasted the
forbidden fruit,
it's irreparable,
you can never quite go back

metamorphosis from reality into image

when I'm
really busy because of
being on the go
the whole time
and the kaleidoscope of my impressions
starts to acquire velocity and
momentum
I start to feel that bit lighter,
less weighed down by that brute weight of a tired environment
which was so wont to surround me

there's less time to stew on the
oppressive sameness of the old man in the moon
but no time at all for relishing right now
because my terrified attention is always fixed on the next hurdle
hurtling closer;
when letting our attention lapse,
psychic torments casts their dark shadow;
so often without reprieve,
so often smashed to smithereens
under the trample of horses;

like a bolt from the blue I see that
my stresses have leached from view,
my attention was so hamstrung
that I never saw it coming
I savour the moment as it enters my being,
takes possession of it,
and recedes,

and when the kaleidoscopic images
project onto my mental retina especially thinly
the world is reduced to a pretty light-show
and I savour the irony

yet should a naughty throw a spanner in
so that the turning mechanism jams
I fear the psychological pile-up
which might one day result

no bogeyman

always a catastrophe appears to lurk
behind everysoever twist and turn
of fate's blow-by-blow vacillations

and so the natural instinct is to spend
every god-given moment fortifying our defences
but it can feel like trying to dig one's way out of a hole
because as a result there's never time to do anything else

but should the soul throw caution to the wind
she's struck by this anti-climactic sense that
every experience is just what it is
and amid the general flux of life it's only transitory;
maybe there's no bogeyman hiding in the wardrobe
after all

we've seen all reality's endless
different permutations a googleplex
times before
and so we're like the ball-bearing
in a hermetically sealed pin-ball machine -
there's never any danger of falling off the edge

other souls

my soggy socks

as I skip
past the puddle
of the aura
of another
the splash on my socks
weighs down my world

now I secretly see
how physics transfigures
the shape of the splash
and the sound of the squelch
into the outline
of a Life

love in the night (original)

I sooth divine,
in the tempest
of existence,
reality just slips and slides,
nonetheless,
all so very gentle
and barely mental
we call it life

conflict pricks and rents
my psychic tent,
cosmic forms
backdrop the storm -
what feels real now
evaporates without a trace
in the tsunami of time

through all this ceaseless flux
it's incumbent to pick up :
the sole psychic guiding thread
is the soul within my head -
through the magnifying glass of mind
it fills this empty firmament

it seems a paradigm of reason
to steer the ship
attentive solely to subsistence
oblivious to the vagaries of seasons

to squeeze another aboard my bubble
would seem to spell me psychic trouble -
to erect a bastion
of my soul's attention
in the life-path

of an independent person,
would seem thus to throw my whole composure
hostage to the vagaries of chance -
yet once I've spied that secret flame
forever after I cannot look askance the same.
Love is the baton which keeps the human flame alight
through the forsaken and eternal night

love in the night (modified, as read at Andrea's brother's wedding in 2012, by her mother)

I search for love
in the tempest
of existence.
reality just slips and slides,
nonetheless, despite the chaos
and the clutter
we call it life

conflict pricks and rents
my psychic tent, cosmic forms
heralding the storm I fought through –
what feels real now
evaporates without a trace
in the tsunami of time

through all this ceaseless flux
the guiding thread
is the soul within my head and heart –
through the magnifying glass of mind
I imagined a light that fills this empty firmament

but just when I thought that
to share my life would squeeze me out,
erecting a bastion
of my soul's attention
in the life-path
of another person,
to throw my whole composure
hostage to the vagaries of chance –
I suddenly spied that secret flame
and forever now I'm changed and cannot feel the same.
For love is the baton which keeps the human flame alight
through the forsaken and eternal night

commentary

This is an existential poem, and while it may seem bleak it is ultimately about hope. To Andrea, the divine truth being searched for was a way of seeing the world, seeking the satisfaction of a life really lived, finding a moment of inner harmony and gentleness in the aggressive banality and "ceaseless flux" of the modern world.

Life itself can feel like a riddle, wrapped in a mystery, inside an enigma. And Andrea was the physical embodiment of this. Her realisation, and the beautiful secret hidden in this poem, was that no matter how dark the night, we are all connected and interdependent. And ultimately it is love – passed from one to another like a never-ending relay race – that enables us to survive and even thrive. The incredible last two lines of this poem should be remembered and oft repeated by us all.

Nick Johnstone-Waddell,
Andrea's brother.

lust

I can't explain this carnal flame
which bathes yon soul
in the soft glow
of a halo
and erects it on a majestical pedestal
all this, in the dull grey of day
and despite my listless and cynical brain

this sexual fire
just mystifies
while breathing life
I can't decide if it strikes from outside
or kindles what's already within
yet a certain person appears so enticing
by dint of my peering from the outside in
e'en though, my reason protests
there's just an ordinary mortal within

while I'm caught in your vortex
I'm living in the instant
and querying my reason
and ever so slightly
unsteady on my feet

spiritual acrobatics in a world of Newtonian mechanics

my soul and hers cut a swathe
through the dense cultural undergrowth normally obscuring
the site of another's soul's terra firma
and as we draw together as if by the most primitive of telephones consisting
of two tin cans and a piece of string
we become oblivious to that universal noise pollution (caused by
people's addiction to talking shit)
drowning out the soul's oomptey-oomp;
it's like our souls levitate and embrace but
it's just a telepathic sense which I can't prove;
at these moments we leave aside talking;

the attention heightens;
the mind falls over itself in its quest to absorb
the perfect sweetness of the situation through the sensory pores,
as I meet her eyes, meeting mine
my soul cranes its neck to better follow
the trail of reflections

it's nonetheless disturbed due to
wretched ignorance of whether this idiosyncratic turn of events
should be destined to continue
or doomed to death

while her spirit cohabits with mine, the otherwise
achingly mundane and ordinary has been metamorphosed
into an intoxicating neurochemical fix

next time we meet, my wandering soul thumps
her head on a newly installed security fence
ring-circling this other spirit, except no longer itinerant
but now holed up in a castle which boasts of all

the latest mod-cons, yet I can only take the press's
word for it – it's like walking and hitting
your head on a lamp-post

she treats our last encounter as if it were
the most unremarkable event in the world ever to claim air-time,
she makes no admission of any such spiritual
drama as I had envisioned to be taking place alongside,
had my whole love-life to date been nothing
but a psychic construction of my fevered brain?

for her it had all been, so she now gave me to believe,
purely ordinary in the sense of means to an end,
just as our taxi was a merely a vehicle transporting us from A to B;
we were merely going about our business as anyone could see
and there was nothing more to be said

but please never let historians of the future claim
that the surreptitious meeting of knees in the corner of the tuk-tuk
was not evidence of a secret rendezvous
between two twin flames

painting the chiaroscuro of love

I know sweet-well the face of love
when basking in the cool and shady compassion of another
yet despite my well-plumbed tap of humble thanks,
I know full-well I'm gazing into the tunnel of the unknown -
for 'tis the character of grace
to flutter nonchalantly in the breeze
brushing up against ones cheeks
without any semblance of Reason,
nor offering up to scrutiny its starting place,
while want of succour doth militate against
all such idle speculation -
hence I'm none the wiser
concerning the length and breadth
of my benefactor's sacrifice

the soul is incapable of loving
the human source whence springs
love's every selfless act
not owing to a deficit of tender feeling
there to draw upon
which it might liberally bestow
but for want of that god-like manna
which maketh the star of knowledge
which alone can fire the trail of Eros

and when we seek regulation
of our everysoever act of grace and favour,
far from hauling love into view,
we merely fête and perfect
the rigid external conditions
defining propriety,
although furnishing a seductive image
all quite useless,
all this, while shrouding the heart from the gaze;

we banish it, under the table, as if it did not exist;
our only tape-measure of love lies missing

in my solitude,
I'm often given to forgetful mood;
in the whirlpool of reflection
I so easily merge with my metaphysical surroundings;
all articles not thereby nailed down
become swept up by this raging psychological tempest
and I lose sight of myself
while the road-blocks to thought
including so many petty gremlins
masquerade as reality
and fuse with the noetic horizon of truth

though driven by the spirit of propriety
the soul enters into most social situations
maintaining some end in sight
while quietly sliding by so many representations of the not-quite
dead
(I might add how we've all suffered under the capitalist's lash)

yet what's paradoxical
is that the perfect social rendezvous
volunteers absolutely no use;
it is merely the opportunity
for the soul to have her existence confirmed
as distinct and beyond dispute;
yet while the group makes no further allusion
her soul vanishes from the proceedings
left to peer down from the ceiling

'tis the flickering, smouldering flame
of the unadulterated life-force
unashamedly selfish
which flags my concentration –
when I'm allowed to see it

I want to marvel at that naked chi
vying with survival head-on

the chance to steal a peek
at this shrouded nether-world beneath our normal schemes of
meaning
depends on a spirit
who can rise above the existential quagmire
to reveal the truth of her spiritual fire -
I can then rejoice in the evidence
of another free-spirit besides myself

I can extrapolate backwards all the spirit's actions
kind or unkind
as springing forth from an ethereal origin
where the soul ultimately resides

merely for the odd glimpse of a man's self-conscious truth
I can forgive all of a soul's so-called "moral" slips
by re-interpreting them all as infernal blips -
I want to understand the selfless sacrifice
as the agonised expression of a fundamentally selfish drive;
compared to mere civic duty
it's so much more beautiful

a token expression of good-will

considered whole
humanity gives show
of such a seething swirling molten mass of souls
such that much as I would wish to honour
the immortal spirit living inside the body
of each human
discrete mathematical unit
which, though a clone, cries "me too!"
I cannot begin to grasp such spiritual vastness
and I can only stop and stare
and wonder at the seething pot
from the Safety of my Lair

yet my emotions billow and surge
in this near-windowless world
humid and close
until I open the sash or the skylight
and marvel at the black of the night
and I open eyes to the fact
that the human community
is a dreadful delusion
quite blind to the metaphysical distance between man
and man

for all of our squabbles
arise from failing to honour
the sacred in each other;
or, by the same token, from the soul's
sheepishly revealing
or venturing to make evident
the very same in herself

yet come, follow me outside
into the gloom
under the stars and the moon
there we'll comprehend the sacred
once
and for all time

---

commentary

For me this is an incentive, a call to arms and open hearts in a war for love and acceptance, a rallying of the troops, to be brave and just try. I particularly love the last wave of the poem "yet follow me outside into the gloom under the stars and the moon". I would follow, I would join this brigade.

Rachey Edwards,
Friend of Andrea's.

to absent friends

the truth is
we pass much of our lives
in solitudinous climbs

yet heaven forbid
I strike a morose note

for we feel touched
by just a clutch
of souls
whose shadows have tickled
the innermost reaches
of our spirits

and if we think about it
we can supposit
anysoever spirit we please
because all-encompassing spiritual reality
is all happening now

yet mark how these spirits
dance hither and thither
before our mind's eye's theatre

to give thought at all
to a spirit
we've necessarily been punctured
by their penumbra

but evidently not nearly so thoroughly
exactly to pin down
how they're faring precisely
now

yet they feel so real
we can't abjure
conjecturing all the details
which we only do
on that supposition they should be true

their soul unfolds
exactly parallel
to our own
for we're all party
to the self-identical unfolding
of time's origami

as a result,
there's a feel in the ether
bearing witness
to the mood of my blood-brother
or sister

and I shadow this imagined frame of mind studiously
through the winding paths
of Father Time

other times, when the life of the spirit I think of
has been cleft separate from my entire jurisdiction
I feel rather invisible

when thanks to circumstances
I can be reunited
with dear beloved people
its just such a pleasure to feel touched
by the dynamic thrust
of the sovereign force of life

commentary

Andrea's passion for literature and philosophy shines through in her poems. She loved to engage with challenging ideas and concepts, her work exploring themes that have concerned many people for centuries: the meaning of life, death, consciousness and the nature of reality, to name a few. However, her poems are also deeply personal and moving, showing the great value she placed in friendship. "To absent friends" touches on the loneliness we all feel in life, at times, but strikes a highly positive resolution – "when thanks to circumstances I can be reunited with dearly beloved people". A sentiment I share with Andrea, who is one of the "clutch of souls" to touch my life.

James Hubbard,
Friend of Andrea's.

the geography of the spirit

I often feel like
I'm living on a metaphysical island
far apart from continental society;
indeed, nothing impresses upon me
quite like the realm of here and now
but it's just a nothing as far as the world's concerned

to make connections with other spirits proves just as tricky,
e'en though the life of the soul is what gives our world its
meaning;
yet it seats them around the outside of its perimeter fence
in nooks and crannies and shadows
and separates them by thick thick jungle in between

ne'ertheless, our world proudly boasts a utopian bent
always promising redemption of the present woe
through the steady march of progress;
perfect succour's ever deferred to a future time
a little beyond the horizon
that's why I judge my look-out by here and now

but surely I am under some illusion,
for the world's just an assembly of individuals
pursuing their own good;
yet if truth resides in the spirit
and not economic cycles
and petty rules
we'll make restitution only by
coming together as a group

scattered as we are
about this planet of ours
I'm still none the wiser as to
whether we all partake
in the self-same present moment
in which case 'twould be sacred and we must
return it to its natural lustre,
or if we abide in disjointed parallel realms
where a particular present is just a psychological fetish
in a meaningless stream of time

but surely interaction is only possible
if we exchange some secret sign
as testament to one common lot
taking place, moreover, before our eyes

the theatre of the absurd

let's take it as an axiom
that it's only pragmatic
not to expose more than a corner
of your spiritual wardrobe
to your fellow *man*
(but you can say what you like to dogs and cats)

hence, when people interact,
as a rule, they're only acting
leaving us none the wiser
as to what deep-seated secrets
lie concealed
behind a person's iron curtain

perhaps everybody is always secretly smug
or, conversely, anxious as fuck;
but going through the same motions
in both scenarios;
but when my father lamented,
apropos of nothing,
"Oh Lord, where will it all end?"
I felt strangely disturbed

when the soul seeks to analyse
this absurdist theatre
she must admit defeat until such time
as she can peer inside other people's minds
or read the secret soliloquies;
until then, there's an artistic licence
to interpret the world however you like

it may be that we're protecting
the softest part of ourselves
like a hedgehog does with her spines;
but we may also be perplexed to know
what we should be feeling or thinking
like a hedgehog who's just avoided being run over

we squirrel away our amorphous spiritual feelings in the soul's
closet
in a kind of Pandora's box
and watch them evolve;
like nuts under the earth
we leave them to grow undisturbed

everything is process
and nothing is ever settled
and the natural state
is to be dazed

the truth about dialectic

oft-times buried deep in the middle
of the conversational ritual
when in perfect oblivion
to the timely ticking of pinions
does it strike me
I've been long since replying
without anysoever effort of trying
or the feeling of combat

thus I revel in the dance
of the conversational art
with yon partner

a psychical nodule detaches inside
so to spectate the exchange
all the better all from the gods
leaving my communications hub just to function on auto-pilot

to be sure, it's a magical feat
how my lips feign to speak
of God and immortality
without so much as a flicker within me -
on the contrary, I'm wholly transfixed
by that film of moisture
adorning your eyeball
eclipsing your eyes
from the streaming sunlight
leaving me to contemplate
what's behind

underneath these clothes, my soul is naked

why are we so scared to face
the world naked?
But on the contrary we must hide behind
a factual mosaic,
which lays claim to a whole host
of assorted trivia and accolades
and it pinpoints our nexus
on the power network

we dream of neatly stacking the facts in the background
of our private redoubt
then cashing them in
for a happiness annuity
at the prevailing exchange rate

when we request the pleasures
of any particular houri from our factual palace
more often than not
we'll be thwarted

I keep shifting my beliefs every minute
'cos I'm at a loss to specify
what I want from life
and in any case
I'm beautiful nude
so what need of shame?
but I know a sea of tranquillity
beyond this god-forsaken mosaic
where the world just falls away
sometimes I catch a glimpse of one of society's foot-soldiers
gazing into the infinite distance

and I know she's swimming in the same ocean
but then she'll quickly gather herself together
and mentally recap the facts about herself
before smoothing out her jacket

---

commentary

It's a magical Sunday after Gay Pride in Brighton. Andrea, beautiful nude, walks to the sea and swims into the breaking waves. Fortunately for the other beach-users that day, longshore drift takes her half a mile down to the non-nudist end. We rush to meet her with her clothes, but pebbles barefoot are surprisingly painful, and by then everyone has gaped in wonder at this cool, 6ft blonde's stunning, lithe-limbed body. O lucky them!

Anna Harris,
Friend of Andrea's.

this human zoo

while my delirious spirit
grapples with phantoms,
other folk give the show
of exceptionally shallow actors -
though it behoves every person
to rehearse a
unique piece
for all I'm concerned each blurs one
into another

if I anchor secure
my imaginary ship
in the fantasy port
the distinctive shimmer
of all sorts of neuroses
is mine to behold

God only knows
what psychical drama
takes place inside folk
in their hearts.

being me

too long I've been seeking
the essential truth of my being.
How I'd walk tall in the knowledge
I knew what life was about
and grasped the business of living.
Absenting this wisdom
I'm just a nobody all at sea,
yet how I crave
to nail my colours to the mast
so to join
the naval arena

all about folk parade
identity-badges
which announce they have crossed
a secret right of passage
and have thereby decided the business of life -
thus they flaunt secret knowledge -
how I wonder does this occultish Masonic club
have basis in fact or illusion

in times of peace,
an ensign carves a sphere in the social arena
in times of conflict,
an ensign flaunts an inner poise
and self-conviction

yet how can I commit
when I see that all identities
conflict;
indeed, when I quiz
the truth of my being
I know there's only a hole

instead of a gem
so needs must I transcend
the particularity
of me,
and I mentally knead the human predicament;
but isn't it just such
we're all cut
from the same spiritual stuff?

yet, I contend, every identity
expresses a facet of humanity,
potential in each;
for all sinner and saint,
straight and gay,
spinster or hitched,
muslim or atheist
are simple refractions
of the single being of reason

while I grasp this truth closely
it splinters between my fingers
and I'm left to sort through the pieces.

more freedom, please

what's beautiful about freedom
is it leaves the question
of what the soul is capable of being
unsettled

on account of the world's misery
its only chance of re-invention
is for all the soul's restraints
to be swept away

of course in theory,
the soul can trample over
all barriers,
given the playground of time without bounds

and much procrastinating,
e'en though she's
insubstantial and flat
to look at

but a living, protean soul
is so much more beautiful to behold

by definition, then,
we don't know what the soul's capable of being;
so we cannot second guess
the size and shape most appropriate
to clothe it

what is living?

I would dearly love
just to live
and forsake philosophy
but the Problems of the World
are such as to extend
to its outermost metaphysical Reaches

other people have the appearance
of Just Living;
should we conceive such
as strategy
or spectacle?

divine the true Essence:
Odysseus of the ocean wave,
between Nadir and Zenith.
The Living Dead -
powerless
logical
indestructible

_____

commentary

And you have shown us the way

Never ceasing to be yourself

Directing the strategy of your life from the warmth of your soul

Recording in our minds your strength, your courage, your smile

Existence, is to live as you have done

And I just want to say, thank you, for teaching me...what is living

Bryan Kaulback,
Andrea's Spanish cousin.

a fable

I'm going to tell you a story
even though I normally just play with metaphors

"I'll look after your bike" said the homeless guy
late one evening, as I rolled up outside the store
 "it's okay, you can trust me"

"I'm sure that's true, but I think I'll play safe" I said
"that really offends me. I told you, I'm different from all the other
beggars"
conscious that this might be the soul of a beautiful rose
just seeking to commune
and that I risked tearing it petal from petal
I proceeded to lock my bike to the post;
I'm not a fool

what it is / to have to work like a nigger

(in dedication / to a special lady)

I asked after her
as a respectful gesture
yet her only thought was
to enumerate her working hours
of late – the start time of the shift
and then when she finished -
they were all either o'clocks
or half pasts

it occurred to me
that maybe the burning flicker
within her feminine breast
existed in a walled-off fortress,
in order to protect it
from the ravages of work

or maybe her being had been
so entirely absorbed by the capitalistic machine
that she sincerely supposed
that the well-being of a working-class black woman
could be read off from the share of her moments
claimed by the white man, and the remaining fraction
in which she was allowed to quietly simmer,
like a kettle always kept on stand-by mode

one of her functions, as ordained by her supervisor,
but, so she thought, ultimately sanctioned by the Almighty,
was to act as toilet monitor,
so that whenever the white man wanted a wee during the night,
she would be there to hold his hand and shake his *****

inscribed in every stroke of her demeanour
was the deference of her forefathers toward the plantation chiefs

her stature, plain and straightforward as it was,
appeared entirely lacking in the white woman's coquetry, but threw
into sharp relief the moral hollowness of the latter's ruses;
yet when God calls my friend to account
how proudly she can enumerate a lifetime's working hours

Anna Akhmatova

some reflections on "A Portrait of Anna Akhmatova":
a painting by Nathan Aldman

stirred from my scrutiny
of the painting my ears pricked up
when they heard an old lady complaining
to her companion that she was getting very
distressed looking at it because it was
full of optical illusions

"it just can't be a true representation
of reality" she opined and she was on the point of
declaiming Nathan Aldman as a fraudster and a liar

she was further distressed that
her companion did not share any of her misgivings,
who merely kept repeating her mantra that
"it's just a difference of outlook";
clearly she was either a secret fan of cubism
or she just wasn't that bothered
and was happy just skating along
on the surface of things

I came across the duo again in the next room
where I was surprised to find Old Lady A
as we could call her, now starting to sob,
and wailing that she was at a loss to know
why the issue affected her quite so much

Andrea Waddell

now an old man came into the picture
and intoned that "it really doesn't matter"
just as he would to a child, when attempting to insist
that the lack of strawberry jam isn't actually
the end of the world

still seeking answers through
her veil of tears, her clogged up voice
pierced through the cloying atmosphere
which had surrounded her
and exclaimed "I'm intrigued by that
one over there" and she gesticulated
towards an arrangement of pieces of wood

but now came the kill, now she turned
murderer, if only words could crush
the soul out of earthly habitation,
that is

"maybe you're not supposed to be intrigued
by art, maybe you're just supposed to stare at it passively";
her companion did not betray a flinch as
her friend accomplished this deft character
assassination

no, she just stared at the pieces of wood,
staying neatly outside the other's field of view;
they were like two men
urinating in two neighbouring urinals,
wanting to make sure they avoided being seen to look
at the other's hose-pipe

I could see lady B itching as six
words playing on her lips:
"it's just a difference of....."
but this time she kept mousey quiet.

commentary

This is clearly personal reportage, a fly-on-the-wall account of two elderly female aesthetes vying for cultural one-up-ness, a briefly intrusive male voice counterpointing their contest (but contemptuously ignored, needless to say). The irony of the rivalry is of course that art is a coded message from the artist to the onlooker, and if your code is different you shouldn't be dismissive, or upset, if you don't get the message. The final simile, switching the gender perspective, provides an entertaining parody of mutual aloofness in conclusion. Incidentally, both the picture and a profile of Anna herself are accessible on the internet, and there are so many points of emotional and experiential contact between her and Andrea.

Robin Waddell,
Andrea's father.

sociology

theory and practice

by right of theory
this world we live in
is so very easy

behold the sprawling web
pre-spun'd
- a bureaucratic wonder!

just skip along
your flaxen prong
till ye find your chosen inn

my privy sensory reports
would mark me down a spoiling sport
yet they pronounce it fit
for solely Superhuman Sorts

(follow-on: Christopher Robin and Pooh / Pyschology)

séance with society

where is she?
… that soothing social oil
greasing that Seething System
we like to call
Society

my mind's eye
frenetically flitted
o'er the humble hovel of my soul
while my substance subsisted
in th' eternal now
of my corner of the cave

where is she,
my spiritual cargo?
In the box labelled – soul?
Buffeted about, I called in the crowd
in the Social Swirl,
the egg-and-spoon sprint
we call
Society

where is she,
th' elusive lady
of Society?
I think I saw her as I snoozed
she beckoned at the door
escorting me
through marvellous mazes
and flights
of fantasy

when Ariadne's thread
stretched to a stop

I scolded my mind
for all further phantasms
Hark!
I sensed the sound
of my soul calling 'supper'!
and I sauntered home for the soiree

Postscript

others, I believe, would gladly elope
with th' elusive lady
of Society.
yet, every time, does the girl
evaporate
in a swirl
all this, hopelessly far from home!

commentary

I immediately warmed to Andrea's expressive and mischievous smile. We spent three happy and challenging years together, studying and overcoming health and housemate issues that would have made your head swirl! I just loved her light, joie de vivre laugh and the way her healthy-living self blended beautifully with her uninhibited, Goddess-like self. We always had a fun and thought-provoking friendship. Whenever she confided in me, she made me feel wonderfully human and valued.

Anna Harris,
Friend of Andrea's.

supernatural strife

"the social sphere's
not far from here"
whispered seraphim
in my Inner Ear.
"Follow your nose
there's a bar in the east
devoid
of dress code"
then softly to my soul, signing off:
"In the social sun
all the world's
awelcome!"

some kindly clipper shunts me from the rear
insodoing, inducting self
in the carousel's spell
the loving lilt of language
lights my way
astray

in our passion for sport
we play the uncombative sort
gentlemanly jest and feminine fun
first and best
it's a choreography of kind
soap-operatic smiles soothe time

in the midst of the melee
at the centre of the stage
my mind contemplates
to abscond
the anthropological party
before the familiar face of Fate

surfaces
fashionably late
hands me my marching order
he gives my psyche a jog
declaims social life as a fraud
so now I spectate from the gods

is the spirit anachronistic?

in these ambiguous times
all's a fast and furious blur
to the casual and untrained eye

the penalty for dawdling
is to take our eye off the ball
and set ourselves up for a spectacular fall

when all's flux and flow
spiritual deliberation on the state of the soul
or idle time brooding on its right and proper good
is thus entirely detrimental and without profit

our distaste for still life
mirrors our surprise
at the way a photograph halts time

we grab hold of each practical fix like a jungle vine
we are urged to turn a blind eye to the accompanying
psychological trip -
we even flaunt a stiff upper lip with traditional pride

what's ironic is that
all courses of action become equally valid
when we affect to distain the effect on the spirit -
for we live in an age of original nihilism -
whether we worship god or the bomb
does it make any difference?
and perhaps we only act at all
from force of habit
because we've done whatever it is countless times before

e'en when we perceive an inner gloom
it gives reason to pedal faster
so as to escape from the dark depths of the soul -
in any case we only truly know
the practical way of action
uninitiated into the occult mysteries of souls -
and perhaps they're just an
epiphenomenon of the material planet

we're far too used to pain
to ever really truly complain
and we set ourselves up as mini fascist judges
and we mete it out to others as punishment
again and again and again

all the time we keep bobbing along
unacquainted with real pleasure and real pain
all of our endeavours remain completely and utterly inane
for we lack any anchoring point of reference
with which to distinguish value and cost

only in suffering is the soul
stripped down to the bone
and thrown back on its haunches -
to grapple with metaphysical reality
is necessarily daunting

we see opened up the chasm
between inner and outer
we crave to partake of the mysteries of spring
and merge with the whole of nature
through the soul's osmosis

yet the soul must both wrestle
with simple existence's necessity
and endeavour to grasp
simple existence's art -
only this way
may the soul undergo
catharsis

we can only know true spiritual fulfilment
when we have grasped its secret foundation
in the way of the tao

---

commentary

What powerful thoughts linger here!
As always, Andrea's word-smithing is pure gold-smithing, rewarding the reader with shared revelations, eliciting: "Yes! That's just how it is!"
She's so right – in this "ambiguous, fast and frenzied world", we must take time to find and ponder our inner selves, whether that makes for peace or pain. Who better than Andrea herself to know: "only in suffering is the soul stripped down to the bone and thrown back on its haunches". Brilliant.

Dr. Peter Little,
Family friend and Nick's godfather.

on freedom

freedom's like a bright light
from which we shield our eyes

for we are wont to feel beholden
to the concerns of the moment
because we're usually enmeshed
in its subjective assessment;
and so we dance to the capricious tune
of desire's rule

but if we seek out
the alien heart of sensation
we can break out of our heads
into the outer realm

it's that place where politics
is made a mockery of
for our rulers persist in laying down
what's right and what's wrong

I can only visualise
different bits of life at a time,
so it's so hard to discern
an idea of the whole world,
yet it's my spiritual horizon

and this is the place to say
that the idea of the global
has been hijacked by our political controllers;
who doesn't lose heart
at the thought of the Pax Americana?

and when we feel politically repressed
this just adds to the tension
for our rulers have means
of making us sweat;
though I most reproach God
for condemning me to freedom

as our mind seeks to soar up
time's leg-irons keep squashing us back down into the mud
and angst again holds us captive

when the ghost of labour
comes make itself felt
and, once again, we commit our pound of flesh
we take refuge from thinking nothing matters
and nihilism's decay and putrefaction

yet when we sacrifice
the ultimate gift of time
we also wind down our minds
till they're just functioning on auto-pilot;
it must be a deceit
if we think this is freedom

how we revel
in the pretence of necessity -
yet when face-to-face
with infinite possibilities
we're scared witless

the questionable merits of the law

I often wish
that the law didn't actually exist,
for it continually teases me
with the possibility of justice

it tingles at the periphery
of every law-abiding conscience -
and in this way can it embody
the very greatest force known
to the psyche –

though nature may shape
the world's building blocks
the law always skulks
in the background,
ready to wield th' power
to crush or raise up

how the law sprawls in the conceptual realm
like a frayed rug
such that the only thing holding together its multifarious threads
is the symbolic power of the law considered in itself

the law rules over our minds
as a pure symbol of fear -
for we dread to test
the chemical reaction obtained
by exposing it to real life

yet when needs must we desire
to harness the power of law
all of a sudden we twig
what a creaking machine it really is;
the faultless image of law
in the water
dissolves among a plethora of ripples -

in times past
when life was short and nasty
'twas easier to accept a wrong
and move on
now justice ever masquerades as just around the next corner
honour dictates it must be sought
at all costs

mark how a law-abiding society lives
underwritten by fear, but not justice

---

commentary

Commenting on Andrea's poems and one in particular is not easy, but here I feel that she questions life, law and justice that we all question but do not want to delve into or disturb. Perhaps we should all look at the good that our 'law' does and the fact that it is outweighed by the injustice of it all, or does it all come down to the old adage that 'life is not fair'? (I am sure this is over-simplifying Andrea's meaning greatly!)

Helen Thomas,
Andrea's godmother.

on Mammon

isn't it quite bizarre
how the money-making imperative
sets all things into perspective?

the shadow of mammon
casts a pall of travesty
over all our petty squabbles
and trivial little riddles

for it's incumbent upon us all
to perform the alchemical feat
of creating something out of nothing
or, which comes to the same thing,
carrying out the confidence trickery
of making a profit

though much reviled,
mammon carries no prejudices;
she treats us all alike

for comfortable living
comes with a price tag –
to be specific
we're talking a fortune

our minds glaze over
with archetypal dollar signs;
it's a realm only comprehensible
through purely abstract figures

yet comfortable living
bespeaks nothing but natural approval,
things are merely as they should

it comes to pass
that we participate
in two quite parallel lives

life bifurcates
into the everyday world of sense,
and a fantasy world
populated by solely money and numbers

our physical endeavours,
squarely situated in the first,
needs must appear quite incomprehensible
when considered of themselves

is it not the shadow
of some lurking calamity
which maintains us in our curious labours?

confronting Christianity

when feeling most bestowed by a sense of
the common lot of humanity
and every living thing
the will most intensely presses upon me
to alleviate
others' suffering

yet it's often as if the assumption of self-gain is what makes
communication possible,
and that a softening of our self-serving demands equates merely
to a weakness of will
and so a mentality of universal compassion
needs must discombobulate
the logic of our squabbles

our air's all-pervaded by the stench of want
such that if we flinch for an instant
from the mind-set of avarice
our liberties are quickly gone

he who sets out on the path of giving
will be sacrificed on the altar of our want
and will be made last in the line
for the inevitable frenzied rich pickings,
there waiting out in the frost
and so left to shoulder
our deadweight of sin

so who's truly ready to follow the example of Christ?

a cautionary tale about drugs

as my way I wend
through the sinuous rills
of nostalgic travels
I picture how, growing up
I lost my dearest friend
to drugs

what I most bewailed
was ne'er making plain
to her
my fondest love

I gently broached
my soul
the fearful notion
that she's ne'er coming back
though I balked to call it fact

well, I shouldn't have fretted
for, as luck would have it, she came back from the dead
and I was re-united with my friend

the friend so nearly
plucked away by evil drugs
whose spirit
was on the brink of
fluttering away forever
into the infinite distance
was none other than reality herself

civilisation and its discontents

the people who run
civilisation always seem peculiarly
sure of themselves that
this is the way to run things;
they are very arrogant

I think it odd that I should
so often be assailed by
existential doubt
yet the people in charge are
supposedly immune from feeling like
this;
perhaps they've been vaccinated

but maybe those officials
who have been awarded large ranches and
prize cattle prods
are secretly afraid of losing them
if they don't conscientiously police their territory

what very important people won't freely admit
is that their idiotic wills
do not express laws of nature;
there are other ways to do things

now even reality's been branded across its ass

one would be forgiven for thinking
that the building blocks of reality
were constituted by brands

and that before
attempting to think a thought
the mind must put at its disposal
the requisite collection of logos

yet behind every brand
lies the cadaver of a once aspiring thought
now tragically consigned to the morgue

for whenever the soul thinks a really good thought
it sometimes comes to pass
that it's plucked from between her paws
and hung out to dry
on capitalism's washing line
and then it's branded
with the farmer's red hot irons

now its home is inaugurated
on the extra-sensory plane
and the mind is tempted away from
its time-honoured world of sense
where it fondly believed answers to be found
in the sky, in the trees, in the clouds

we may imagine
a numinous presence or aura
clinging around the brand
enclosing the logo
but perhaps it's black magic -

how it tempts thought into its brightly coloured layer
there demanding commitment to five-times a day prayer -
how the brand dresses itself up
as some kind of signpost on the way to paradise -
yet surely it's a recipe for getting lost
if we subcontract thought to the multinational conglomerates

the uncomfortable fact is that
the riddle of existence
must be thought afresh every single instant

in this poem I will pull no punches and tell you how it really is

behind the optical illusion
that the state will always look after you
and behind England's best traditions
of Fair Play and Cricket
the soul senses that ubiquitous dread
which segues from living
it's as if she's precariously poised
on a tight-rope stretching far into the void
in both directions
she knows all too well she has to look after herself

clearly any time that is spent
away from learning and usefulness
is colluding with the void
and beckoning death

yet when I attempt to plot
the arc of my life
I realise how many years I have lost
to the virus of television advertising
and that all that I ever learned from it was how to line the pockets
of the adman's designer trousers
(not that I've been tempted to help him out)

a theory purporting to explain why we eat chickens

the reason we eat chickens
is because we know we won't get locked up for cannibalism
and because Jamie Oliver does it

(see also: a dedication / the nature of the artistic endeavour)

my anarchist poem

the system has each individual in its grip -
she's instructed in her role as a steel-rimmed pinion -
yet the grand machine churns away
without an ounce of purpose;
it merely asks that we perform our jobs
without any heed of the consequences

the system disdains
any appeal to our spiritual centre
because it boasts a tangled web
of self-regulation;
and only operates on the plane of logic;
and it would dearly love to replace its human beings
with machines

within this mania for professionalism
other people's private existences
have been decreed off-limits;
and so with no community of souls
there's no opportunity
to construct something of value

our heads are a blank space
ripe to be filled with rules and regulations
and so these are the only terms
in which we're permitted to think

there's no reward for following orders
except to be swallowed up
by the societal behemoth;
one will then regard the shadow of injustice
with deep-seated puzzlement

yet should we be judged to fall short
of obedience to orders,
it will bare its fangs
and digest us front to back
in an act of reverse peristalsis
allowing us a tour of the system's deformity first hand

---

commentary

As Anarchists go, on first meeting, Andrea was a pretty unlikely one. She did a very good turn as a dizzy blonde. Defying stereotypes though, she was a true free spirit, one whose passion drove her to see the value in the liberation of others.

Ben Hawley,
Friend of Andrea's.

be very angry

it's incumbent on the soul to be inconceivably angry in protest
against the system which would steam-roller her out of existence
as proof that she is still very much alive and kicking
and refuses to have her very emotions
legislated and made suitably insipid

for anger can never be neatly swept under the carpet;
yes, it can punished, but it always leaves a stain
on the minds of those establishment lackeys we rail
against, which seek to suppress the incipience of a conscience
as they battle insomnia

the machine seeks to grind the soul down
into the dust of nothingness
in its desire to perfect itself
through this war of attrition against loose wiring and splinters

its method is to deny that she ever existed in the first place,
except, implicitly, on the very ethereal level of power relations
where our socio-political encounters
are nothing more than the acting out
of a game

the rival psychosities look down from above
on this childish game of poker – stroke – snakes and ladders
whose ultimate prize is unimaginable wealth
and whose penalty for failure is degradation – stroke – death;
now and then we cast our eyes
onto the inscrutable gazes of the other playaz

in the calculus of conflict
pain is not a permitted variable to be negotiated with;
it's just the psychical remainder
from our social relationships

the natural world

back to basics

I know a still small place
where the world just floats -
the landscape of experience
just takes place:
midwife to all
new life,
in the nascence of sensation.

please picture those many things
so wanton to bestow
their many shocks and blows -
now nothing can evade
my eagle-eye'd gaze

in the shadows do I hover
ever hawkish to a twinkle,
though the merest premonition -
as I ponder
shifting shapes
as they constellate in space
(though a new-found natural wonder)
each must declare itself afresh
friend or foe
else I embed further
and more securely in my hole -
then the ripples will dissolve
the reflections in the pond
so foreboding

in this world of ghosts oft-times besieged
I authorise, by course, what comes in, what may leave
ever on the qui vive
lest a trojan spy-horse

by her siren sound-track
infiltrates my sacred cave
so to wreak its wide-scale havoc -
spirits loom large, then bounce back
leaving me shaken
yet unscathed.

yet in my sequestered mental work-shed
this army of objects
has infiltrated my defences
and colonised my mind
to co-habit in my mental dell
each leaching my attention
debasing my awareness
resulting in this mindless, fuzzy mess.

when I meditate upon this suffocating landscape
I recollect each gift-horse
came emblazoned under auspices
of a little slice of paradise
on condition this hermit left her still small place
to dote upon her new-found babe
- until all autonomy of thought was gone
yet the stench of cadavers remained

with a little upheaval
can I retire to the cradle of nature
with nothing to make claims
which weigh on my attention;
instead do I behold
naked life
taking place -
for the world just floats
in my still small place

psychic symphony

how the clip clops
and the schwuur schwoars;
how might I speak
when my senses find themselves
already spoken for
in sound

and the tattle tittles
in its Twisted Tongue
this smorgasbord of Sound
Corrupts my Consciousness
ensnaring me in studied stupefaction
dissipating brain in purdahed putrefaction

but beyond the bish of the bash of this sensory soup
- this occultish hors d'oeuvres -
I suffer a simmering storm;
oh how my psyche shivers
at the surrounding siege
of this Tsunami of Silence

though my corporeity is calm
canalised through conscious confinement
in the court-yard,
outside there assembles
the spiritual spectre
of my social situation

oh how this silence gently writhes
with rotten riddles,
teaming with these tremors
of interpretation,
before back-sliding
to the Silent Slime
and the beautiful bird-song
and the buzzing of bees

the joy of squirrels

yet how I give myself up
to the spectacle of ducks
(always reassuring)
and surrender to limitless pleasure
when I surreptitiously glimpse
the shenanigans of a squirrel

hence I'm left confused
why I so often fail to feel enthusiastic
over the spectacle of the human

if I squint
I descry the gossamer threads
which comprise society's cobweb
beyond the inner-life of my head

it's a picture of persons
getting ahead
and making their way
with that gay swagger
of old-fashioned abandon

yet beneath
the hustle-and-bustle of people
faithfully serving country and crown
lurks the shadow of power
faintly shaping the palpable space
of my living existence

this tangled web envelops us all in its goo
such that all I perceive at the top of the tree
are not squirrels
but agents of darkness
against me

my affair with the floor

how I mourn for the time
when sticks and stones died;
'twas the adult religion
which consigned my dear friends
to th' inanimate kingdom

when I was small
how I cherished the floor
and looked up to the walls -
from the tips of my fingers
I revelled in the logic
of physical thinghood

now I'm taller
the floor and I have grown apart
I've learned to shun
the material order

inbetween, intercedes
the whole complex code
of this grown-up globe

now the physical jungle is never quite real
it's just the cinematic backdrop to our psychical film,
a mere mental diversion
from professional haste
to the litany of tasks
at the political rock-face

there we mine ethereal meaning
for the king
with no clothes on

the body

at the risk of boring you
I'll tell you a little story
about the contents of my head
and its connection to my body
but by Zeus I know
that this is where you'll want to be

when my mind is feeling
dizzy
from the whirligig of
living
and it's tired of parsing
the sensory inundation
of senseless information,
I can't help speculating
the universe's stated reason
accounting for the brute fact of
my existence

without doubt
the tale pleads ins and outs
but needs must cul-
minate in
here and now

so what's important
is here before me
in the form of
my physical body

I sport a variety of organs
and body parts
including legs and arms
all bristling life

each component piece
is suggestive of a function
which desires exercising
and taking care of
but it's all a fiendish code
which I can but try decipher

when body parts fall short of
proper working order
thus disrupting my whole composure
I'm left perplexed,

and as for adjudging
what might behove
the body's ultimate function
or over-arching role,
other than securing thoughtless bondage
to its own eternal worship,
I've no idea -
the logic of my senses is
truly tested to the brink.
So is the body just god's little joke
just like all those pre-historic bones?

commentary

I met Andrea at the University of Sussex where we shared a house with three other students. I have a vivid memory of Andrea, a result of many conversations in which she usually settled our discussions with one or another wise ideas.

Her health was not optimal but she was never a complainer. At times she talks in her poems about health, the lack of it, even death, as well as the struggle to summon our will power or find inner quiet. In most cases it was her preference to point out the silliness of a situation or make a humorous remark as when she wonders whether the body is just "god's little joke just like all those pre-historic bones" or when she notes that although you cannot establish the existence of gremlins, it is easy to perceive their work in certain circumstances.

Carmen Cacho,
Friend of Andrea's.

stealth of the weather

my mood always feels
as god's private judgment solely upon me
oft times mine own tragedy
or good fortune -
I duly banish my mood
to the empyrean realm of my attention
for it swells upon the crevices of my head
all by itself

unbeknownst to the integrity of my spirit
'tis curious how the weather doth contribute
to the unique quality of my mood -
yet I presume that all other souls
pay heed to solely rational protocols
and only thus can the social order tick

yet mark ye this; the seasons are stalking me -
and by gentle turns my mood is transformed diametrically
and it dawns upon me that the weather must be declared guilty
whilst I had blamed heaven and the frailty of my will -
then again, if heaven doth dwell high in the sky
maybe heaven and the weather are single

'tis curious how other souls follow the seasons
like the clockwork of fashion -
yet I can't help feeling it's all a bit superficial
for I'm quite oblivious to any existential misgivings deep within
them
but other times I exult in a profound Sense of Togetherness

but yea, when we all worked the land
how we respected the seasons like gods

my psychic exposure on the heath

as the winds crash above my head
I puzzle how such outer mayhem
can instil such inner peace;
perhaps the forces of cacophony simply cancel each other out
and each elemental voice is drowned out within the meaningless
babble of the crowd

I revel in a giddying spin
and as before me the fenland whirls
I feel necessarily endowed with the strength of Atlas
to fling the fenland full-circle thus

the roar of an air-plane hurtling through another place
and the steady whooshing sound of cars on the motorway,
all so soft yet replete with symbolic pointing,
conspire to give me horror of this fragile paper-thin void
and I feel a deafening silence
transpiring within my cranium;
yet I determine to delight
in the translucency
of my *tablula rasa*

as my body revolves
I chance upon a blot
which has made its station
on the fen atop

as fate would have it
it's nothing other than
Southern Electric's Agent of Death;
better known as
an electric pylon

I crane my neck
to digest this Babel;
and so peruse the contents
of the accompanying sticky label:
"5000 volts: danger of death"

I note that the Grim Reaper has solicitously provided
a trail of grotty nails that one might climb
from fen step by step up to embrace the end;
this study in logical neatness
has now sullied
my once untroubled inner peace
and one-ness with the heath

---

commentary

In this powerful poem Andrea writes of man ruining the natural beauty of the heath and the inner peace she could have found there. I have a memory of Andrea in harmony with her surroundings, in a beautiful unspoilt cove in southwest Ireland. Striding into the sea, she began to swim with her wonderful strong strokes. Soon Andrea was a small dot heading fearlessly towards the horizon, the bay curving around her.

Here she seemed to have found a one-ness with the ocean.

Julia Walker,
Cousin of Andrea's.

a letter to the all-powerful machine

oh great machine godlike, invisible
yet situated in our very mists
so far above the heads of
any individual man, yet demanding its obeisance
from every one, not that it bestows any
reciprocal favour onto the great lumpen masses,
excepting the likes of some CEOs

just as your deep sinews are greased
with that dirty black glutinous gloopy fuel,
and let's face it you always did err on the dark side,
and lacked the hygiene standards of upper-middle class
housewives
it powers too your tireless thrashings
and zombified manoeuvres,
yet not dreamy but performed with the crazed
application of teams of orcs

I know you scoff at the hippie battalions
who set up yoga classes in their furrowing wake
everywhere they go, and witter on about karma
and converse wistfully about the after-
hours tai chi and qigong sessions
scheduled to take place in the next world

how they proselytise
everywhere they go about their beloved wind
turbines and recycled chicken shit and
fantasise about a giant hamster
running round in a big wheel
which would power all the squats
all around the world for eternity
they crave renewable energy

because eternity speaks
to them of god and beauty,
and they always were too stupid
to comprehend the flaw behind
any perpetual motion machine

you have even been known to chuckle lovingly
at the sheer naivety of these witless ingenues
but the true anarchists get swallowed up
by your hungry coal-fire furnace
before it spits them out as pollution

there are others who are so enamoured
by all the beautiful stuff which the filthy oil
produces that they keep salivating and
craving more, craving more
just like they're faced by a luscious joint
of veal. Though they know it's wrong,
they crowned their appetites as sovereign

they exist in an opium-induced
slumber and are oblivious to the filth circu-
lating inside their veins,
they're in denial too of that moment
of time stalking closer,
sometimes plodding, on and off, tortoise-like,
other times scampering like a rabbit,
when cold time-honoured reality shall again rear its head

oh great machine, do you not shed
a tear when you take pause to consider...
but perhaps that's difficult or impossible
when it's all systems full speed
ahead and you're risking gazillions of juggling balls
so artfully choreographed till this present juncture

coming crashing to the floor....
surely you understand its days are numbered;
we're scraping out the final barrels

in which case we may
be witnessing the death throes of an empire;
but in the event of apocalypse comrades please
check for alterations
to your local yoga-class time-table

but make the switch to wind,
sun, tide, geo-thermal, and shit
in time and your machine may judder on unperturbed
dispensing your worldly injustice
until, perhaps, either the masses rise
up in revolt or Christ returns
or even the dinosaurs

time

meditations on time

they say the past is dead and buried
each moment hallowed
for single use only
in the structure of the whole -
blink and you miss it -
each dark chapter of the past
consigned full-faced to the dustbin of history
or filed away till judgement day
but so many times in life
the shadows of the past do resurrect it
as if from nowhere they rear their head

what's further, if we merely rearranged the tables and the chairs
who'll dispute
we'll be re-living ancient affairs
over again?

how I write off dim memories
well and ill
as picture post-card snaps
their once pulsing life
which did augur of the future
slipped between my fingers
in the crumbling sands of time
such that I can no longer distinguish
what's real and what's illusion

yet they say of here and now
'tis the face of reality's finest hour
even the whole being
of the blooming existential flower
or wilting lily

yet 'tis recurrently the case
the present has an emptiness
while I try muster faith
that the manna of life past
will spin again about the carousel
to bring us face to face again
but just as plausible
that centrifugal forces
will fling my vital sustenance
hurtling thither
into the bowels of deepest, darkest, outer space

tomorrow as the start of the rest of my life

as time advances, like a tsunami,
wiping out all that's prior
it endows the now with its arrogant flavour,
but the corollary is that
the now exists in an unstable state
always ready to sacrifice itself to that which comes after

to imagine we can transcribe reality
into a "state of affairs"
suggests over-optimistic arrogance;
it's a theoretical fantasy

until time packs its bags
and goes home
surely everything will be fluid
and changing

but how much patience is required, on the contrary,
to chart the unfolding of any scenario
in real-time

if time is just the resolution
of an unfolding logic-puzzle
what little value can we give
each moment as it passes
except as the notes in the margin

commentary

This poem fills me with such hope and positive thoughts! Do not dwell on the past for you cannot change it, enjoy the here and now by doing what makes you happy, and look to the future but not obsess over it – what will be will be! Each day is a gift but a small thread in our beautiful and colourful life tapestry.

Charmaine D'Rozario,
Friend of Andrea's.

summer-time delirium

when I give recollection
to the persons whom I've met
each embedded in events
it feels as if each happenstance is still occurring
in a sealed-away room
in some dusty far-flung moon

in the throbbing heat upon my pate
precipitating down
within some strangely privileged god-given here 'n' now
where the mundane world boasts
an undeserved splendour
and one is given to the devilish suspicion
that nothing is
quite like it's rendered

each alternate version of reality
doth compete for ascendancy
on a strobe-lit rota
whilst, in the blink-blink of an eye,
I lose all recollection why life should be blessed with
here and now not there and then
and even cognisance of which is which

we cast our sight
full beyond the seas of time
upon truth's immutable horizon;
we plant the goodness of our souls
as a bulwark 'gainst erosion,
and just for a moment
we stand defiant
before the ceaseless March of Time

the only action that can be taken
is to wheel out long-lost acquaintances in cages;
yet there remains the unanswerable question
as to what use could be put
the cadaverous remains of the dead

---

commentary

Andrea's poems take you on a journey through a verbal maze to arrive at an insight of what it meant to be Andrea. At times reflective, at times desperately honest, you catch a burning glimpse of the shining spirit within that fragile shell.

Quenton Steele,
Family friend.

Pamplona

we slither and slide
into the night's unfolding reams
like zombies

ever propelled by
the magnetic force of Father Time
yet we would imagine some more glorious
end in sight

sometimes we hitch a lift with
some institutional cruise-ship
which, though founded on lies,
allows us, temporarily, to sit back and enjoy the ride

whilst our mind is otherwise occupied
the fluid of time can flow away
and the natural processes of renewal
are able to take place

sooner or later we're always forced to confront
that the purposes of the world are all for nothing,
which leaves us with boredom's riddle
and the recurrent suffering of existence

we've always cause to put faith
in the wisdom of nature
but when confronted by decay and death
we'll give it the benefit of the doubt
if we have reason not to end it all now

we've been condemned to the necessity
of filling our time somehow or other
so we're always striving to stay ahead of ourselves

but we're always being stalked
by time's creeping forces
which singe our tails
if we slack off the pace -
it's like Pamplona's bull-run

the prodigal son

as I weave my way
through uncharted spaces
the past is wont to seem far away

each present moment
invariably shocks me
with its novel quality
such that everything hangs
in the balance;
one path points up to the Elysian fields
the other down to Hades

however much I've veered from
the beaten track
I'm often prey to the experience of déjà vu;
then I feel as if I've chanced upon
a hallowed sacred space
where nothing changes
and which can be relied upon
to always stay the same

then the intervening period
feels like a trompe l'oeil
as if I were merely walking backwards
down the up-escalator
and for a moment time feels like
no more than a trick of the mind
before I swerve once more
into the thick of the jungle

vivisection

I'm desirous to pin down
not only who am I
but what constitutes the substance of my individual life
though I'm prone to doubt
whether the issue can be ironed out

oft-times I treat life well bespoken by the moment
whether said life be
cluttered up or,
when fate should be so good,
more simply hewn in moon or sun

or when in pensive spirit,
I envision it
made up more roughly
by the trail enfashioned
along life's passage

when, due to stress, I curse my evanescence
I grasp and clutch at existential ballast
"my memories are all I have,
it's who I am",
I tell myself

the mental process of the past
is wont to avalanche
upon the now
leaving me e'en more incarcerated
than before my jaunt

yet memories are elusive booty
- for they're not all found
beneath the garden bower -
it's only when engaging
miscellaneous pursuits
that forgotten memories are triggered
and different forks of memory lane are picked

no longer can I trace a single line
of what should constitute my life
no longer am I lacking one single self
I've unearthed more than twenty-seven,
which is disturbing

each memory is tinged with
either values which fulfilled me
and infused a sense of purpose
or, failing that, ideals which I admired
but found lacking
in myself -
yet pursued them nonetheless

when taken unawares
by a sense of yore
I oft mourn for
unfulfilled life-courses

yet how may I determine
which life I am living,
which life is alive and kicking
and which doth lie dormant

déjà vu

I live a life of heightened sense
and frantic thought;
etched deep down
inside my feverish temperament
lies a lusting after more

what's seducing me
of late
is this crushing weight
of immediacy
and chasing fate

though I hate to bore,
this feeling gnaws
of déjà vu
it's high above the ceiling
it's deep within my sinews
as if this id's
been here before

if I squint
I catch a glimpse
of other presents
they're sepia-tinged
so real and yet
so strangely flawed

as I gaze aghast at idle dreaming
I'm cast adrift once more
to anxious scheming

thought

thursday thoughts

these thoughts
coruscate the psychic sky
flashbulb flares they fill the firmament
each cerebral scout
searching
for the Way
Out

these thoughts
spit and splutter; they
hit their heads
on celestial clutter.
Each psychic dart
sacrificing self
to the Puzzle
of the Promised
Pasture-land

these thoughts
fizzle and flop
all looks like a leisurely lull,
a mental road-block.
In fact from the flanks, do Satan's snipers,
(under guise of materialist matters)
secretly slay
my thoughts for the Day,
like clay pigeons
they Shatter.

these thoughts
leap like lemmings
to death's daring denouement
sending shrapnel to the skies
scratching my spectacles
and also my Eyes.

truth and delusion

how it tires me
to reconcile
the twin-tasks of my conscious mind;
my duties include
seeing things as they are
and ne'er to slip from positive thinking

my soul acts as a magnet
drawing all thought
to the pressing business
of the present instant

a positive mind-set is requisite
if I shall have reason
to act at all
rather than just wallowing
in the sameness laid down
by the status quo

yet rarely or ne'er
does this positive gloss
simply transfigure things
into its own mould,
e'en so the weight of reality,
so accustomed,
makes itself surely felt

thus I feel constantly stretched
in two opposing directions
between the intellect's
will to truth
and the life-giving will to delusion;
it's akin to the rack, that medieval instrument of agony

yet when I draw back
from the exigencies of the instant
for the first time I behold
the world beyond the confines of my soul,
and I witness the splendours of the natural world
and I see the beauty in truth
and I observe the dominions of other living spirits;
in this way I seize a little vital perspective
on the life of my id

---

commentary

Andrea teaches us through her own personal struggle. As her life unfolded those around her were blessed with her empathetic nature and pro-active attitude. In her journey through this life she shows us hope and success is possible.

Maya Woodit,
Friend of Andrea's.

roller-coaster

one thing I've learned
through life's other-worldly flux
reality just twists and turns
it's a struggle for my thinking reflex to keep up

in the whirligig of life
just sit back enjoy the ride
(how I wish there were a cream for treating
atavistic mental itching)

when happiness deigns drop by
my-oh-my, it's like literature come to life!
We drink the cup of liberty
We feast our eyes
Become drunk
And (for want of prosody)
Just sleep it off.

how our thoughts chaotically whiz
in the blizzard,
come alive
just in time
for the Poet's Recital.

when the snow comes down to settle,
thinking's weary
but it's itching more than ever

de profundis

profun-
dity is quite a drug
all said and done
yet securing my supply of it
is never fun
it's just a drudge
when I crave an instant hit
thinking flails in scrubland sticks

time time again
life's sense of necessity
throttles my penchant for reverie
till my soul is half-dead

I send out a whistle
to my soul's analytical
twin-sister
but there's only an echo

I remain vaguely aware
that life ain't set in stone
yet my critical thinking
remains far, far, from home

thought's often imagined
as the force that drags forward humanity -
to be sure,
when I was small
and I said prayers in my head
   after climbing into bed
I thought my monologue meant I had a hotline
to God's cochlea

now do I suspect
such inner deliberations needs must simply reflect
on a feverish temperament
and bear witness to the curious feat
of me talking with me

such uncalled-for self-absorption is wholly distracting
and imbues my thoughts with the character
of the sea monster Kraken

thoughts scud along wild and unbridled, heedful of nothing
it is, as 'twere, they were riding bare-backed on a buffalo bucking

as such times of cerebral ferment
I do long
for nothing more
than the peaceful tranquillity
of a head empty of thoughts

the zen factor

when bore-
dom opens the floodgates
to the ecstasy of thought

suddenly I'm tumbling arse over tit
into thinking's bottomless pit;
I'm so utterly ensconced
by the mind's objects
that the rest of reality is blotted out;

I'm just like King Midas,
but everything *I* touch turns to ideas;
even when it fails to dismember
the perplexity at life's centre
I can never escape thought's mire

how I'd love just to bask
before a thought like a work of art;
yet thought's only kept alive
by continual exercising;
once I put it on a pedestal and stand back
the daisy-chain falls apart

then I'm at a loss to remember
the content of my reverie,
yet if I squint I can glimpse foot-prints in the sand
beckoning I retrace their steps
like the haunting notes of the Sirens;
or I can plod on with life

the artistic endeavour

broaching the limits of poetry

I must confess
the normal living-state
to be an uncomprehending daze;
for as far as the eye can see
it's all surface and no meaning
which maketh the mind's eye glaze over;
and wherever it finds a prickly bit, its gaze retracts inward;
thus I'm confined to a flat landscape
described not by poesy but by prose

yet the poet in me
wants to roam freely
planting unlimited flags
all about the mental landscape
like a gung-ho imperialist;
yet what she's really seeking out
and her heart's craving after
is artistic uplifting
and the epicentre of doubt

so should this metaphysical East Anglia
be walled off
as a no-go area
for the aspiring poet?

yet as soon as I puff
on a cannabis roll-up
my questioning hound
breathes into being
and suddenly nothing is out of bounds
she'll sniff where she pleases

and as I thump
along the ground
and the wave of vibrations
makes my skull shudder

thoughts are sifted
through the mind's sieve,
and from time to time dislodged
from a barren precipice
until they emerge
fully formed in the conscious world;
it's like collecting the booty
in a fairground amusement

yet I may take no credit
when inspiration strikes
for the muse always takes me
by surprise

poet's block

4 walls enclose me
exposing me to the hum of the clock radio,
muting the night's thunderous rumble.
Next door the gentle hubbub simmers -
to think, I have nothing to say
alas but it has been said
and still anguish racks my body,
my soul too.
The night sleeps.

wild-child

my poetry's gone out of control;
it's laid siege to my entire skull;
now whenever a thought it thunk
it has to be in a rhyming couplet
except in this case, of course, a triplet

I go to bed scheming
about stressed and unstressed syllables
I'm quite sad, really

the secret

when I ingest my favourite authors
I feel the comfort of a secret bond
which pours scorn over the separation
of time and space
even if they're long gone

for their understanding of life
as observed from within
is indistinguishable from mine

and henceforth I feel carried
through life's darkest spaces
by a guardian angel

he's looking down from his cloud
or perhaps from sideways
or perhaps now I've assimilated a vial of his chi
we share the same body

-----

and through any interaction
if I feel we both appreciate the same secret
and play by the same rules of the game
I feel touched by an incandescence
and nothing else matters

other times it's confusing
to know if we play by the same rules;
for when I sort through the shrapnel
I want to find my dignity intact

however can one flourish
and society get by
if we all play by different rules?
perhaps a solace from alienation
is in writing

somewhere down my 'to do' list

I quite fancy regurgitating
the novel inside me
no doubt stuck somewhere down my windpipe

I'd draw on my real experience;
there'd be no point in constructing imaginary hopes and fears
and implanting them in stick persons;
the only novel I'd want to write
describes my journey through this life

but when I consider the matter plainly
I can't work out where it would need to kick off,
without perpetually regressing;
birth is such an artificial
place to start –

and it's beyond me to determine
where it should draw to a close
for with my life in a perpetual state of unfolding
I'm yet to identify the story's moral

---

commentary

Andrea's story was meant to emerge. She was like a flower, gently unfolding through this incredible journey of life. Where should her story draw to a close? It doesn't have to.

Andrea teaches us through her own personal struggle. Ever insightful, she repeatedly challenged fear within the "perpetual state of unfolding" pages in her amazing life journey, her empathetic open heart and mind revealing kindness, love and courage. Joyfully, bravely, with heart let your own chapters unfold, live your story.

Maya Woodit,
Friend of Andrea.

all the spirit needs is paper and ink

how the soul fancies herself as writer
ever striving to spin a bonnie tale
from the disparate threads of life

but god never stipulated
that life had to unfold
like a novel;
if such were the case
then we wouldn't need the creative imagination
of Tolstoy

and in view of life's paint-spattered aspect
we're normally tied up with what life throws at us next
so that mulling over the connecting threads is just a distraction
from the task in hand

and when fate goes crazy with the secateurs
suddenly there's no story to tell
and what story ever existed
evaporates in the mist
or gets lobbed in the bin -
for after all, god never decreed
that life must be meaningful;
it's as if the soul dashed off the train
forgetting her manuscript

other times, how we endeavour to bind ourselves to the past
just for the pleasure of keeping alive a ripping yarn -
but we'll never forgive and move on
so long as the past is endowed with logic

I like the feeling of going on a trip,
but perhaps its truth is a fiction

commentary

What struck me was the repeated imagery of life as fiction. It's a "bonnie tale", a "manuscript" and "a ripping yarn". Our lives are a story we write ourselves and that ultimately we are responsible for our own story.

Her final line is " but perhaps its truth is a fiction", and reminds me that it's not my place to judge someone else's life. There were many who judged Andrea by the newspaper headlines her death provoked without knowing of the "disparate threads of [her] life". Through these poems we glimpse part of Andrea's yarn as she saw it at that moment in her life.

Anne-Marie Stevenson,
Andrea's aunt.

nervous twitch

I've spent my whole time alive
upon this interstellar rock
collecting evidence
about how the world operates

I fancy authoring the ultimate political treatise
but each new experience sets the world in a different light
and the possibility exists that I'm just slow to learn
and so my treatise will prove to be pointless and superfluous

I keep scheming about doing a work of fiction
which contains a representative depiction
of how things really happen on this planet
but I can never quite transcend the experience of me
as I never quite did get other people

so in the absence of a full set
of operating instructions for living
on this wandering orb
I've assumed the brace position
and I'm holding fast
for that eureka moment so beloved of Chinese
Zen-Buddhist Rice Farmers
but I'd hate to get interrupted by any sort of abrupt end

the optimal existential state
is a little bit twitchy
because though the soul is at a loss to find a logical basis
for choosing one path over another
she's driven by the fear of choosing none;
the only other alternative is just to feel dazed

and so she enmeshes herself in a web of future ventures,
each one resplendent with beauty,
which she can never quite touch -
just like Tantalus condemned never to be able to reach his fruit -
and her sense of well-being plods along behind
like a faithful canine
just so long as she never pauses to scrutinize her
because her happiness will vanish
just like Eurydice did when Orpheus, overcome by anxiety,
climbing out of the underworld, looked back
to confirm his lover was really there
in defiance of his promise to the gods

so perhaps our sense of well-being so far
never actually had any connection
to the soul's vacuous projects,
so perhaps our future welfare shall
meander outside of our control,
but perhaps we'll maintain that illusion of being in charge
right to the bitter end

art, my saviour

I just want to remind you
that art's offices
always maintain an open-door policy

such that however far down degradation's oesophagus
you may be gazing,
just like Jonah, inside his whale,
you can always cackle at the prospect
of degradation and death
with the undying Spirit of Tchaikovsky;
and as the clouds burgeon
she may even spit you out

and let Mussorgsky give vent
to your delightful triumph over adversity
with his requisite combination
of crotchets and quavers -
and some minims

and the music of Rachmaninov
is always playing in life's background as a soundtrack;
only our spiritual ears
are usually too weak to pick it up
without the help of a radio-aerial or cd-player,
unlike those of some ants

it's truly a paradox
how we can lift ourselves out of any fracas
into art's heavenly stratum
thence to look down dispassionately

I just want to caveat
that particular curators may
impose particular constraints
on museum opening times,
but don't blame the paintings

Andrea Waddell

reading a sentence of Proust

how the crowd hushes
and holds its breath
as you hop, skip and jump
from one set-piece routine to the next
via a multitude of dog-legs;
and as you twist and swerve
I can see a figure in the crowd mouthing
'where's the subject, where's the object, where's the verb?' -
for the integrity of your edifice
may hang on an unremarkable single word
so easy to miss
in the midst of your verbal fireworks -
but then you ease to a stop
with the merest fleck of a round dot -
and the crowd erupt into ecstasy,
and the judges spring to their feet
brandishing placards reading
Ten, Ten, Nine Point Nine, Ten

a writer's skill

I am not an alien
I am not a barbarian
I am not a penguin either -
doesn't this character description
just come to life before you
in this very room?

a dedication

I love all of my readers
and all those who come under the sway of the dominion of reason
but a little known factoid
is that my poems are also for the chickens and the cows;
I love you too

---

commentary

This poem is so Andrea.

I write as Andrea's blonde hairdresser – Our darling, dizzy Andrea who could only have been blonde!!

Whenever I watch "Friends" on T.V. Phoebe always reminds me of Andrea, so if you want an Andrea fix please watch it!

Much love, Tina, xxx

is it poetic justice?

if the content of a poem
had to be proven before a political tribunal
there'd be no more poetry

occult

the games of fate

when my spirit's driven
to imprecate 'gainst the iniquities of living
and thereby garner all the pleasures accrued from being
dismissive
and I fancy launching myself out of the quotidian into orbit
with my crack of the whip;

in a lucid instant
I wonder whether life is just the neutral reality
in which we float and pursue our multifarious activities;
or if it's something else,
to wit, a game which is being played at our expense;

and whether or not
we're in the lap of the gods
the origin of life was obviously no regular phenomenon
which painted life a peculiar stain
on the physical landscape;
yet it's my opinion
we're being toyed with
because life's so habitually tainted
with the interference of fate

yet whenever we sense
some supernatural event
the memory immediately begins to fade
until it's consigned to time's landfill-site
and we prefer to doubt that it ever took place

and when reason hits a stumbling block
despite every appeal having been made to logic
and reality's functioning

appears to have hiccupped
it's easy to perceive the work of the gremlins
though in the final reckoning
it's impossible to prove if the gremlins exist or not

when a person is plucked from the public
to rendezvous with us
it's clearly a miracle that it's this particular individual;
yet we're blasé enough
to let them seep back into the crowd,
perhaps gambling on the possibility of another encounter

and fate is accommodating
with a spurt of chance liaisons
before she sucks this person
forever back into the masses,
never again to be heard of -
I can almost hear fate's cackle

while fate marches apace
we're left navel-gazing
searching for some rhyme or reason
driving the persons we meet,
whether it's to be love at first sight
or, including both at the same time,
ships who pass in the night

passing time

when my eyes clasp
onto another soul's artichoke heart
I can't help
but believe whatever she tells me
and lap up whatever words she exudes
and store their general sentiments away
in a cranial vault marked 'true'

but with time's passing
their once lustrous divinity appears to tarnish
and I feel like I'm sweating their particles out
through tiny microscopic stoma
in my soul's lining

sometimes I get these vibes through the ether
or tremors through the earth
which have the shape of thought waves
that another soul couldn't help leaking
though their appearance
may be sullied by my own mental interference
and on occasion, when I'm tired, I even feel the flutter of fairies
circling hither and thither through the air-conditioning

I can't help speculating further
whether these tremors are a product of my own
over-excitable neurones -
and how often I fill this spiritual silence
with all my doubts about these absent souls
but these might be just a product of my own insecurity
and period of solitary confinement

thoughts on karma

in traditional human practice
we're taught to do as we would be done by
or, if we won't
we'll be done by as we did;
but is the rule lifted
in the case of our conduct towards poultry?
for we can never be a chicken

and does the rule fail to apply
in the case of a vicious tyrant
who knows he will never be on the receiving end
of his appalling crimes?
but then Saddam Hussein
seems to have miscalculated
so then the question begs
whether we will ever be reborn in a chicken shed.

---

commentary

This is a massively thought-provoking poem, all who read it should contemplate its meaning. I believe passionately in past lives and karma, all too often people act with no consideration or thought for others. The way that Andrea highlights this is brilliant! It should make any reader contemplate their own actions in their every day life, not only concerning animals and their welfare but also how we treat each other and our planet.

Charmaine D'Rozario,
Friend of Andrea's.

the spice of life

it would be ever so nice
to sup with the gods;
there in a toast
to imbibe
the secret of life

or, eavesdropping the banquet
fathom the motivating springs
behind the scriptwriters'
heart-strings
which we earthlings experience
as unfathomable logic

absenting this spectacle
I cower in my vestibule
tip-toeing 'twixt and between
the clangs of man's
rationalising itineraries
and logicising judgment
- just blindly feeling for the firmament

when osculating misery
I brandish mild perplexity
e'en defeat
till, in a tea-break from eternity,
the gods haul me to my feet

when anaesthetised by love
I give supplication to above;
thus do suppose my road
to be sanctioned
by Olympus
Now emerges all creation
with its seductive cobweb
of temptation

the pattern

we spend our whole life
in the grip of astral patterns
which can't be detected by the naked eye
but can be confabulated by the mind's
construction site when it plays "join the dots"
right up to the present moment but beginning with birth

the pattern
can seem like a random agglutination
of events which only exists in the mind in any case
and not in the outside world

we can excavate no law of nature
which insists life has to unfold in this particular fashion;
even the perception of fault lines
is all in the mind

whenever we exercise our velleity
the domino effect set in motion can boomerang back
upon the unsuspecting homunculus

still we want to think we create
our luck because the goddess fortuna
smiles gaily on a positive attitude

but whatever the outcome we look eager to
extend the pattern's reaches
and we can't escape the pernicious image
of fate at her loom, weaving and brooding

rendez-vous in Samarkand

we're always poised equidistant
between health and degradation's bottomless pit

& everytime we feel the chill wind
of the destructive forces of entropy
even if it's just a pang of hunger
sooner or later the will must come over all heroic
even if we decide first to finish our game of croquet

for the further we let ourselves tumble
the further the will has to claw ourselves back up
and we see no other possible objective
in life than to smooth the path of our will-power

when the demands of rolling the rock back
up the cliff get too irksome we long to be able to wash our hands
of it

even death can seem just a chimera
such that the descent into the pit
might seem like it could be endless;
so we always have to haul ourselves back up

no doubt death will tease us often
before it will grant us permission to desist from
willing

commentary

During the long nights when pain kept sleep at bay, alone in her Brighton flat, I imagine Andrea must have often felt herself disintegrating from "the destructive forces of entropy". But she would heroically summon willpower to "claw herself back up" the cliff.   In this poem I find a strong hint that she is depressed (not surprisingly, as depression is another symptom of fibromyalgia) and is tired of the ongoing ill-health.

But Andrea always managed to "haul herself back up", and enabled her strong optimism and the essential sunshine of her soul to shine through.

Sonia Waddell,
Andrea's mother

glossary

glossary of unusual or challenging words used in *Sounds of the Soul: Adventures in Time*

word or phrase   **meaning or interpretation (as used in the poems)**

(nb prefix A signifies a word newly devised by Andrea herself)

abjure	to solemnly reject, disclaim or swear off something
abscond	to run away secretly, especially to avoid punishment
absurdist	deliberately ridiculous art, or theatre, to parody and mock real life
accolade	praise and acclaim, especially by award of an honour of some kind
agglutination	a mass of stuff congealed or stuck together like glue
aletheia	the philosopher Heidegger saw this as open connectivity between the truth of things
amorphous	without any definite shape
anachronistic	from a completely different time or era than its surroundings or context
angst	acute, indefinable, sense of anxiety or indecision
annuity	a regular income in return for an initial sum of money paid
anthropological	relating to the study of human beings and their culture
anticlimactic	finishing in a disappointing or ineffective way
A anysoever	anything whatsoever
apocalyptic	relating to a Doomsday ending of the world
Ariadne	her thread enabled the Greek hero Theseus to escape from the Minotaur's labyrinth
arrow of time	the unchangeable direction that things happen in science and life generally
ars vivendi	the art of living satisfyingly

Andrea Waddell

artefact	something made by someone, or inevitably caused as by-product of some event
atavistic	an emotion (or impulse, or action) coming from primitive instincts
athwart	a sailing term, meaning across the direction of travel
autonomy	independence, freedom of self-government
avowal	an emotional declaration
awol	a military term, meaning temporarily absent without permission
axiom	a reasonable basic assumption which can't be proved without assuming something else
bastion	a military fortification, or someone defending strong principles
behemoth	a gigantic creature or organisation
beholden	indebted or morally obliged to someone
behove	to be appropriate for someone to act in a certain way
bent	an enjoyable skill or interest
bifurcate	to split into two different directions
burgeon	to develop and flourish successfully
cadaver	a corpse, especially in medical situations
capricious	impulsive, changeable, unpredictable
carnal	sexual without love or emotion
catharsis	a liberating or purifying emotional experience
caveat	an advisory warning or caution
chariots of fire	old-fashioned poetic image of dramatic divine force
chi	vital energy in Eastern medicine
chiaroscuro	the interplay of light and shade in a painting
churlish	resentful or grudging
clipper	an exceptionally fast nineteenth-century commercial sailing ship
cochlea	vital part of the inner ear, connecting to the brain
cognitive	relating to how the brain converts sensation and information into feelings and ideas
confabulate	to talk together, to create narrative together

conjecture	to make reasonable guesses or suppositions about something we don't know for sure
constellate	to make into clusters, like groups of stars
coquetry	romantic flirting or teasing
corporeity	tangible physical existence, embodiment as matter
coruscate	to sparkle with light
crepuscule	old-fashioned word for the period of day immediately following sunset
cubism	style of painting initiated by Picasso in which you see several sides simultaneously
deadweight	an oppressive burden
definitive	unequalled in quality or authority, a benchmark for all the others
demise	death or termination
descry	to see by looking carefully
detrimental	having a harmful effect on something or somebody
detritus	a random mass of fragmental decayed remains (animal, vegetable or mineral)
devil's advocate	somebody who deliberately argues to the contrary to battle-test a point of view
dialectical	harmonising two different points of view by smoothing-out their differences
dictum	an authoritative statement or arrogant assertion
diktat	a decree issued by a dictator or conqueror
dint [by dint of]	a specialised word implying virtue, eg "Her success was by dint of very hard work"
discombobulation	a state of muddle or confusion probably caused by somebody else
disingenuous	diminished truthfulness, esp. by pretending to be more naïve than you really are
disparate	totally different in quality or quantity from others in the same general category
A distain	well, not sure, maybe to disdain, or to remove a discoloration
diurnal	happening regularly during daytime, or at least on a daily basis

	Elysium	in Greek mythology, where good people go after death, though not where the gods live
	Elysian fields	Elysium is most frequently referred to as the Elysian Fields; an agnostic euphemism
	empirical	based on experiment or observation rather than theory
	enfant terrible	a brattish person in polite company, behaving unconventionally and being indiscreet
	entropy	a universal number constantly increasing as time passes and things crumble & decay
	epiphenomenon	allegedly secondary to reality eg "mind is an epiphenomenon, brain is the reality"
	Eros	the mythological Greek god of Love, equivalent to the Roman god Cupid
	evanescent	fading away, transitory
A	everysoever	anyone, or anything, whatsoever
	exigency	a very urgent, or very demanding, situation
	existential	relating to human existence, or to existentialism (a rather negative philosophy of life)
	expurgation	editing out, or expelling, the offensive parts of something
	extrapolate	to guess at something you don't know, based on the things you do know about it
	factoid	an unreliable fact based on unverifiable sources or urban myth
	feign	to put on a pretence of some emotion or interest
	firmament	the complete expanse of sky and starry heavens around the earth
	flux	a flow of something, or turbulent change in something
	Fortuna	the Roman goddess of good luck
	fracas	a noisy quarrel or brawl
	garner	to gather or store something, as does a farmer with his grain
	genuflect	to bend one or both knees to something holy
A	gloopy	thick, viscous and glue-like, or temporarily twonkish
	glutinous	viscous and sticky

googleplex	an unimaginably large number : a google is 10^100, a googleplex is 10^google
gremlin	an imaginary imp supposedly responsible for mechanical or electronic problems
guttural	spoken from the back of the throat
harpy	a Greek mythological creature, having a woman's body but with wings and claws
haunch	the hindquarters of an animal
hephaestian	relating to Hephaestos, the Greek god of fire and blacksmiths (like Roman god Vulcan)
hermeneutic	relating to the interpretation of Scripture, or of the purpose of life in particular
hermetically sealed	airtight
hither	towards this place (where speaker or narrator is)
homunculus	a fictional miniature human being in alchemy or early biological ideas
horse-whispering	establishing a natural rapport with horses, especially wild or traumatised ones
houri	a nymph in the Islamic paradise
id	as told by Freud, the subconscious mind containing the primitive human instincts
idiosyncratic	to have uniquely personal characteristics
incumbent	down to the subject person to do whatever it is
inexorable	relentless
ingénue	a naïve girl or young woman
insipid	bland, lacking in flavour or excitement
internecine	mutually destructive or deadly to both sides in a conflict
liminal	at the lower limit of sensation
lumpen	dull, stupid or unthinking
lustre	gloss or shine, especially of a jewel or ornament
lustrous	having a noticeable lustre
macho	tough, masculine, swaggering
Mammon	a false god in the New Testament, personifying wealth and greed

mantra	an unthinking slogan in popular usage or business-speak
masquerade	a festive occasion where masks and costumes are worn, an elaborate pretence
metamorphosis	a complete change in something, as in tadpole to frog, caterpillar to butterfly
metaphysics	the branch of philosophy attempting to grapple with the nature of external reality
methodology	the organised procedures by which some complex task is achieved
militate	to (impersonally) influence strongly against (sometimes for) something
minimalism	art, especially music, using the simplest elements to the best possible effect
missive	a letter, especially a formal or official one
module	a self-contained subunit of something
multifarious	having many parts of great variety
mundane	ordinary, humdrum, boring
nadir	the lowest or deepest point of something, rock-bottom, the pits
nascence	birth, state of being born
netherworld	underworld after death (eg Hell), otherwise the world of society's underclass
neurone	a nerve-cell
nexus	an interconnection centre in a system
nihilism	a belief that nothing, even life itself, has any value or importance
noetic	relating to the mental world, especially the intelligent thinking side
numinous	having a deeply spiritual or religious quality, mysterious and awesome
obeisance	deference, a respectful gesture
oblivion	state of forgetfulness, or being forgotten, or both
obverse	the front side of something, such as the heads side of a coin
ocular	relating to the eyes

	Odysseus	a Greek mythological hero, famous for his resourcefulness and his adventures
	oesophagus	the food-pipe from the throat to the stomach
A	oomptey-oomp	gentle brassband background music in our inner world
	opine	to express an opinion that …
	origami	the ancient Japanese art of paper-folding
	osculate	to kiss
	osmosis	the energy-driven spread of fluid through a barrier or membrane
	Pandora's box	In Greek myth, the First Woman's casket from which all evil came, but Hope remained
	paradigm	the perfect example, or stereotype, of something
	pari passu	in equal amounts, or at least proportionately
	parse	to analyse the grammatical structure of a sentence
	penance	a voluntary self-punishment for a sin or wrong-doing
	penumbra	a partial eclipse, in which the shadow is less than complete
	periphery	the outside boundary line, or surface, of something
	peristalsis	the muscular contractions of the digestive organs that push their contents down the line
	pernicious	harmful or deadly
	phantasmagoria	a dreamlike medley of images, real and imaginary
	phantom	a ghostly, or even imaginary, image or mental symbol
	plethora	a large or excessive number of things, a super-abundance
	pinion	the junior partner in a gearwheel relationship, having fewer teeth than the other wheel
	pragmatic	approaching issues in a practical rather than theoretical or ideological way
	preamble	an introductory statement
	prescient	correctly anticipating events before they happen
	primordial	existing at the very beginning or earliest stages of time
	problematic	causing a difficulty

	problematise	cast constructive doubt upon
	proselytise	to convert people from another religion to your own by means of a campaign
	prosody	the study of poetic structure
	protean	readily able to change from one shape to another
	protocol	an agreed form of behaviour, communication or negotiation in official business
	psychical	relating to supernatural events, possibilities or capabilities
A	psychosities	I'm not really sure !
	qigong	a health-giving Chinese technique of breathing and exercise
	quagmire	a swamp, a hopelessly tricky and embarrassing situation
	quintessence	the most concentrated inner spirit of something, its spiritual DNA
	quotidian	occurring every day, commonplace
	realm	originally a royal domain, nowadays any major area of involvement or interest
	recalcitrant	strong-headed and disobedient
	recap	short for recapitulate, to summarise or restate a story so far
	redemption	something which cancels out the guilt of wrongdoing
	redoubt	a fortified position or stronghold
	reflux	distillation and recondensation
	reverie	an absent-minded daydream
	rill	a small brook or stream
	river of Lethe	in Greek mythology a river in Hades causing total forgetfulness to all who drink from it
	Samarkand	like Timbuktu, or Shangri La, or Ithaca, somewhere we all yearn for inwardly
	sasquatch	in Canadian folklore a hairy manlike beast which leaves huge footprints
A	schwurr schwoars	this rails against the predictability of association and things doing what it says on the box

	scrutinise	to look at something and examine it very closely and carefully
	scrutiny	close visual examination
	segue	stretch away from something like pieces of music played without a pause
	sensibility	emotional depth and responsiveness
	sequestered	unfrequented, secluded, lonely
	seraphim	angels of the highest rank in Christian tradition, though not in Judaism or Islam
	sinuous	graceful, snake-like in movement, or like a waveform moving across a screen
	skulk	to move stealthily and lurk in the shadows
	soliloquy	speaking your thoughts aloud in a theatrical way, especially when alone on a stage
	solitudinous	being or existing in solitude, though not necessarily in a lonely way
A	sombering	having a deeply serious, even melancholy or gloomy, effect
	sooth	old-fashioned word for sooth (as in the word soothsayer)
	spinners of fate	in Greek mythology, they controlled the thread of life of every mortal from birth to death
	stoma	a microscopic breathing pore on a plan's surface, letting atmospheric gases in and out
	stricture	a severe criticism of somebody
	stupor	dullness, lethargy or even semi-unconsciousness
	subjective	purely personal perception, emotion, thought-process, or prejudice
	subsistence	a life-style geared to whatever necessities are available
	subvert	to undermine or sabotage a person's loyalties or belief-system
	succour	help or assistance, especially at a time of extreme distress or difficulty
	superfluous	more than is necessary or required
	supposit	to adopt or integrate something into ourselves, to take it on board wholeheartedly

surreal	dreamlike and bizarre, mixing the everyday with the unreal and impossible
tabula rasa	clean slate, without mental baggage of any kind, as new-born infants are (allegedly)
tai chi	a Chinese system of light exercises and coordinated rhythmic movements
Tantalus	in Greek mythology, was punished by fruit and water being always just beyond reach
tao	Chinese concept of the basis for things to exist and events to happen
terra firma	solid ground
theophany	a visual manifestation of God, such as the burning bush or the pillar of cloud and fire
thwart	to frustrate or successfully oppose something or somebody
translucence	semi-transparent, allowing light through but only partially
travesty	a grotesque imitation in mockery of something or somebody
troika	a group of three people in power, or in charge of something, maybe dictatorially
trompe l'oeil	artistic, decorative or architectural special effect to create an optical illusion
tsunami	Japanese word for a massive tidal wave that sweeps inland and causes destruction
utopian	relating to a hopelessly idealistic state of government and social harmony
vacillation	indecisive fluctuation in somebody's determination or intended course of action
vacuous	mindless, dopey, devoid of sense or meaning
vagary	erratic action or behaviour
velleity	the lowest possible level of interest or intention, a wish or urge too slight to lead to action
veridical	previously dreamt of, or revealed in dreams or hallucinations
vernal	relating to springtime, or occurring during spring
vestibule	a lobby outside a office, or small antechamber
vial	an old-fashioned word for a small bottle, containing some costly liqueur or medication

visceral	relating to bodily organs (especially intestines), hence to deeply instinctive intuitions
wanton	lacking in self-restraint, immoral, vicious, or destructive
wiccan	relating to the modern cult of pagan religion and white witchcraft or Druidism
wont	habitual practice, accustomed tendency, to do something
zenith	the point in the sky vertically above somebody or somewhere (opposite of nadir)

Ingram Content Group UK Ltd.
Milton Keynes UK
UKHW021134230323
419044UK00007B/266